ADV

IN BLUE

JOHN WEBER

FOR MIKE & ANDREA
HOPE YOU ENJOY THIS —
IT'S ALL VERY TRUE —
JUST THE FACTS MA'AM,
    JUST the FACTS

        FREDDY
AKA: JOHN WEBER

ISBN:098530300X
ISBN-13:978-0-9853030-0-6

To: The families of our heroes.

A BOOK BY JOHN WEBER

Celtic America Books

ACKNOWLEDGMENTS

Sam Patrick
Robert and Louise Collins, fellow adventurers

PREFACE

"You ever had to shoot anyone before?" is a popular question cops hear all the time. As a retired cop, I could write volumes of stories about the horrifying and heartbreaking things I've seen and had to deal with, but you can watch that on television every day. What people don't always see or read about are some of the bizarre and fun adventures cops have on the job and the silly and surprising lengths they will go to in coping with the chaos they must deal with everyday.

These are just a few stories of the many adventures of my interesting career as a cop. The names of these folks have been changed to respect and protect their privacy.

First of all, I can honestly say that I have lived the life of a hundred men. It seems like if something exciting was happening I was either in the middle of it or nearby to witness it. I was a hard worker not because I was a hard worker, but because I loved the work I did...at least when it didn't involve people's innards exposed or dead people. I was a good cop for the most part, but I was never afraid of getting hurt or being killed... never. This bothered some cops who were certainly more sensible. Those kinds of cops wear three guns and all the protective gear known to man. You sometimes can recognize them by their black leather driving gloves and the sunglasses they wear when the sun's not out. They also will huddle together and spend hours planning how to go into a house that is under siege by a ten year old boy with a water pistol while the house is burning. I wore a ballistic vest on a couple of rare occasions, only because it was extremely cold on

Foot Patrol and I needed more insulation. I never claimed to be a smart person but I still think I was a good cop, at least most of the time.

I believed in following S.O.P. (Standard Operating Procedures), but generally common sense ruled for me and sometimes you have to adapt to a diverse world of endless scenarios to stay alive. When criminals start to follow our S.O.P's then I will too, was my policy. Besides, I always agreed with that old cop phrase, 'It's better to be tried by twelve than carried by six'.

Working in the trenches of life has its good and bad points. You're bound to take some dirt home with you. Your eyes, ears, nose, and mind take in some things that are difficult to process. I occasionally have difficulty blocking some of those terrible thoughts from my mind and they haunt me. Life keeps me going though, and although I don't miss those ugly moments and the politics of police work, I do miss the adventures. Every adventure was something new. Twenty- three years of looking for trouble earned me some trouble as well, but I'd do it all again for the sake of the thrilling endeavors I was able to encounter and the people that I helped and made smile.

Anyway, *when* these stories occurred isn't clear since I'm terrible about keeping dates in my head, however, the facts and the faces are clear in my mind...so here you go.

THE SCENT OF BLOOD

CHAPTER ONE

It was my first day on the job as a full-time police officer and I was assigned to work with a crusty veteran cop who should have retired years earlier. He was the typical doughnut in one hand and a hot cup of coffee in the other kind of cop. Like many of the old veterans, he avoided calls to keep from having to do all the boring paperwork afterwards and there was always the risk of being sued or even worse, going to court. He was built like a sumo wrestler and I was told that he had been known to throw a full-grown man across a room during a bar fight with one arm while dragging another out the door in a headlock. Somehow, somewhere, someone dubbed him with the nickname of 'Lumpy.'

It was the first call of my first day. Life was good, it was sunny and warm and I was excited. There had been a stabbing in an old seedy hotel-apartment building in the downtown area and the suspect was seen running away. My partner, Lumpy, and I arrived shortly after the call and as we hurried to the entrance of the old building I could see blood flowing out onto the sidewalk from the main entrance. Looking inside the lobby doors I saw two people lying on the steps halfway up a flight of stairs. They weren't moving and it was very quiet. The bodies were a young man and woman that had both been stabbed multiple times. There was a massive amount of blood still pouring from them, actually cascading down the stairs. I never realized until that moment that blood has an odor, a thick, pungent musk that is unmistakable.

'Tex' was a K-9. He was a big, powerful, and highly trained German Shepherd with a beautiful orange-blonde coat with those famous German Shepherd black and brown markings. Bad guys and hostile crowds feared Tex for a good reason. Tex would have eaten them alive if his handler, Officer Jenson, would have let him. On some occasions that did happen, but those are for good stories coming up later.

Officer Jenson and Tex showed up quickly and before long they were on the trail of the bad guy. I stayed behind to secure the scene and listened to my radio to monitor the hunt. It wasn't long before Tex had found the weapon a few blocks away. The attacker had tried to ditch it during his flight, but not only was Tex a good biter he also had a good sniffer and shortly after finding the knife, Tex led the cavalry directly to its owner. I always enjoyed hearing Officer Jenson calling for the medics after Tex had hunted down a bad guy. Tex got a little justice for everyone even if the court system sometimes failed.

The knife turned out to be a medium-sized butcher knife with a wooden handle. The bad guy was a nut case that had become infatuated with the young lady who he didn't even know. The twisted man apparently couldn't stand to see her walking with some other guy and snapped, like the tip of the knife that broke off when hitting the bones of the poor young couple's bodies. I remember standing at the foot of the old hotel looking at the blood drying in the sun and thinking, "Wow, my first call, this job is going to be quite an adventure."

LEARNING THE ROPES

CHAPTER TWO

Some of the most basic and natural abilities you are born with fly out the window when you are a new cop. Walking, talking, listening, and trying to make sense of it all, doesn't actually make any sense for a while. 'Boots,' 'Newbies,' and 'Rookies' are just some of the titles that green cops will answer up to and these new awkward *'Bambies'* stand out easily too. Rookies are the ones that wear the clean, crisp pressed uniforms with the spit polished boots that have toilet paper stuck on the bottom of their heel. They are the ones who come to your window after they stop you only to find their patrol car rolling away because they forgot to put it in park. A Rookie is the cop who has to break into his own patrol car after he locked himself out during a traffic stop. Of course this always happens when the patrol car's overhead emergency lights are still on attracting the worlds' attention.

Multi-tasking takes practice. For instance, making a simple traffic stop isn't so simple. The first protocol is to let the police dispatcher know who you are, what you're doing, and where you want to stop the motorist. Cops not only have to know exactly where they are at all times, but they must also know where to stop a motorist safely. It sounds simple on paper, but for a Rookie it's like landing a commercial jet on Interstate Five in downtown Los Angeles during a rush hour and nine times out of ten the person they are trying to stop doesn't end up where the cop had hoped.

After totally screwing up communication with the dispatcher, the officer has to turn on the patrol car's overhead emergency lighting. Most patrol car consoles are full of buttons, toggles, knobs, switches, sliders, and colorful lights, and the trick is to know what device you have to flip, push, or pull to make those lights go on. Some of these gadgets are useful, some are important, and some are very important.

After untangling the radio microphone cord from the stirring wheel and dropping it on the floor while at the same time flipping, pushing, and pulling every gadget until the lights come on, the officer now tries to stop the car safely. That means the violator and the patrol car need to end up in a safe location somewhere, and as I mentioned before, this rarely happens. Most people don't practice being stopped by police officers and can be as clumsy and mindless as the Rookie stopping them. Yielding in the middle of the road blocking traffic or landing on top of sidewalks are as good as any locations to sign a ticket.

After the Rookie has parked the patrol car and untangled the radio microphone cord that was wrapped around his leg; after he has picked up the paperwork that fell from the visor and wiped up the coffee that he dumped all over the console; after he has turned off the siren that wasn't suppose to go on, he can finally proceed to get out of the patrol car to contact the violator.

Making several trips back and forth to his car to get the correct violation codes, the Rookie now has the poor motorist flustered enough to sign the ticket. Sending the confused motorist on her way, the Rookie gets back into his car only to realize that he forgot to give the violator her driver's license back. However, this is only a temporary and slight inconvenience since the violator was a local person the Rookie could easily return the driver's license to, or so he thought. It would have been best, though, if he had realized the last name of the woman he cited for a very minor infraction had the same last name of the chief of the police for the precinct he worked for.

Microphones on police radios can be a cop's best friend or their worst nightmare. Using the police radio is a challenge for every Rookie and even sometimes for the old pro. Phonetics is used for each letter such as, 'Adam,' for 'A', 'Zebra' for 'Z' and so on. Everyone knows who the Rookies are as soon as they hear them 'on the air.' Rookies often make up their own Phonetics to fill in for the ones they don't know and I made up some goobers that were probably illegal according to the F.C.C. standards. Thanks to citizen-owned police scanners, thousands of ears are listening each time an officer pushes the button on his police microphone and they hear all of our blunders.

A pretty young Rookie female officer volunteered to work undercover on a sting one nice summer day. A male 'flasher' had made several visits to a local park and he obviously had an eye for pretty young ladies. Wearing civilian clothing and carrying a hidden portable radio and handgun, the undercover Rookie was to walk through the park hoping she could catch the flasher up close and in action. The patrol division was made aware of this project and was standing by just outside the park in the event the pervert was caught. It was my good fortune to be working that day.

At first I didn't realize what all the whispering was about that was coming from my police radio, but then I remembered the sting operation at the park. I put my ear closer to my radio. "I think I see him, he's walking my way," the Rookie whispered to the Radio Dispatcher. Of course, not only did every police radio in the county receive the transmissions, but the rest of the 'Scanner World' was listening as well. Her voice was excited, nervous, and yet a bit brave. "He's coming closer, I've got my eye on him," she continued. Her voice was growing more excited and pitchy. The ears of every patrol cop on duty tuned in closer with anticipation. A few seconds went by and then suddenly the radio cracked with the sound of the Rookie's frantic screaming, "Aughhh, he's AuuggGHHHH, GGgggg, Beeeeeeee, Aughhhhh, Zzzzeeeeeeee, (garble, garble)." This went on for some time. Every cop in the county reacts quickly to the sound of another officer in distress and every cop was on the way to the park.

There are some things one should never do after making a fool out of oneself. That is, you should never explain your error in full detail, especially on a police radio. While an army of police officers were arriving at the park to save her, the Rookie's voice was finally heard back on the radio. Trying to catch her breath and gain some composure she announced, "I'm okay. The suspect was getting close so I tried to hide in the woods alongside the trail. I walked into a bee's nest....I got stung pretty bad but I'm okay."

If my memory serves me correctly, the pervert was never seen again. Go figure.

As a detective I was assigned an unmarked sedan that had fake license plates and a hidden radio. I had been partnered up with another detective on a homicide investigation that required working around the clock for several days. Both of us were delirious from sleep deprivation. We were trying to locate a key witness who was a young woman that worked as a strip club dancer in a large city about thirty miles away. The search for this 'professional dancer' led my partner and I to several adult bookstores and strip clubs. I drove while my partner rode shotgun and kept me entertained with his many life stories. Some of his stories and jokes were pretty crude, but I found them entertaining at the time and the laughing kept me awake.

My undercover car's hidden radio was below my seat and it had a long cord for the microphone that I often left laying on the seat beside me…you can probably see where this is going. The problem with police radio microphones is that when you press the talk button you can't hear any incoming radio traffic. Not even if that radio traffic is important and your sergeant and police dispatcher are urgently trying to tell you that your microphone is stuck on.

My partner and I had been sharing our crude stories and laughter for quite a while before my cell phone started buzzing in my coat pocket. The call was from my police dispatch supervisor informing me that my radio was transmitting. Upon receiving the bad news from my police dispatch supervisor, I immediately cut off my partner in mid-sentence and simply pulled up the microphone to his face, he knew right away what the phone call was all about. We realized that he had been leaning up against the radio's microphone and keying the transmit button on. At that awkward moment both of us were going over in our minds the crude things we had said in the last 30 minutes relating to the matters of adult book stores and strip clubs. And then we remembered how powerful my car's radio was and that it could be clearly heard by thousands of listeners, even outside our county in between and beyond. We were dead ducks!!!

The dispatch supervisor told me that the clear give away to the identity of the radio offenders was the sound of my own laughing. Apparently my laughing was more familiar to dispatchers than my own voice. That is probably a good indicator of how much I loved my job, but unfortunately, I didn't have the last laugh on this occasion.

After returning to our office at the Detective Division, my partner and I received an award winning, lengthy, and ear-burning chat from our lieutenant. His vocabulary was much more graphic than anything my partner had shared on the radio and nobody was laughing.

It was the rigorous determination of several good mentor officers who went beyond the call of duty that I admired, and it was their zeal to solve crime that I found contagious. They were the cops of days gone by. Some of them were 'old school knuckle draggers' and some of them were 'quiet thinkers' who would rather talk about fly fishing in Montana than their valiant feats of bravery. They were colorful tough men who were full of spit and vinegar, wisdom, and loyalty to their oath to protect and serve. In my first years as a Rookie, I had the honor and privilege to work with a few of these *real cops* and I was like a sponge soaking up every bit of their knowledge that I could while they were still there. They are all gone now. I believe the violence and the trouble we have in our cities today is a testament that we need those kinds of cops back on the streets.

Whether it is a Rookie officer fighting off bees or the crusty veteran detective unknowingly hosting an X-rated police radio talk show, the learning curve for cops is actually a circle. You never stop learning. Life's variables are endless. A cop has more potential to be a zero than a hero and it's only by determination and growing thick skin that keeps cops on the job. Fortunately most criminals are desperate and most desperate people make mistakes.

It's the mistakes that criminals leave behind that lead cops to their door. Sometimes it is as easy as the burglar's deep footsteps in the snow that tell all and lead the cops directly to their door.

Sometimes it's not all that easy, and the next few stories describe the determination it takes to catch the bad guys.

THE QUEEN OF THUGS

CHAPTER THREE

When I first started working as a police officer I was a Warrants Officer for the first year. I averaged 3 to 4 custodial arrests a day and never had one bad day. Because I didn't have the duties and responsibilities the regular road officers had, I was constantly loaned out to many of the specialty units such as the Narcotics Task Force, the Harbor Patrol, the Detective Division and other specialty units.

I was assigned an unmarked sedan that looked like any other civilian vehicle, but it had a racy motor and hidden police radio. One morning I was on the way to work when I noticed a young man hitchhiking. I didn't make it a habit to pick up hitchhikers, but he looked harmless and the weather was bad, so I figured I'd give him a lift.

I kept my uniforms at work so I was wearing civilian clothing and looked like any regular Joe. The young fellow hopped in and I asked him where he was going. "Down town." he replied. "Great," I said, "me too." The very next words out of the guy's mouth were, "Boy, I'm glad you picked me up, I have outstanding warrants for my arrest and I was worried some cop would see me."

What immediately came to my mind was how I would explain this to my boss. The young man went on to say how sharp he was for avoiding being arrested by the stupid cops. While I was wondering what to do with the wanted man sitting beside me, he asked me where I was going so I told him that I worked down town. He asked me, "You're not a cop are you?" I laughed nervously and replied, "Yeah, right." He asked me where I worked and I told him that I collected garbage for the city, which was sort of true.

Somehow I talked the foolish chap into walking to the front counter of the police department with me with some story I concocted about having to pick up a paycheck. Some people just don't get it. He even seemed surprised when I placed him in handcuffs and led him into jail. I'd bet a dollar that he never mentioned to anyone how he came to be arrested by the Warrants Officer in his own hometown.

During my tour of duty as a Warrants Officer I was asked to assist the Narcotics Task Force in an investigation that involved an organized drug ring led by a very slick woman. Ms. White owned a retail business as a front for trafficking large volumes of cocaine. She was known as the 'Snow Queen' and lived in a small palace in the country. She also had a platoon of heavily armed thugs that kept vigil over her palace. The Snow Queen conducted business over telephones from her bedroom which was her fortress. She never came out of her bedroom so the drug unit wasn't having any luck obtaining a warrant. The paranoid drug dealer certainly wasn't letting anybody into her space uninvited, so the drug unit had to come up with a good plan.

The plan was to get an informant into Ms. White's house and the only way that could happen was if the informant knew Ms. White and she trusted him enough to sell him some cocaine. There was only one available candidate that we knew of who could do the job. The trick, however, was that he currently was an inmate in an out of state prison and it would be difficult to get him released and back into our state. But somehow the drug unit along with the prosecutor's office managed to pull this off with the deal that the convict would get reduced time from his prison sentence if he came through on his agreement with the prosecutor's office.

My part in this wild adventure was to go with the informant to the house and hopefully be invited in with him to witness a dope deal first hand. I had to do this while keeping one eye on the convict, in case he got cold feet and hit the road, and my other eye on the dope deal.

The drug unit's intel found that anyone going into the Snow Queen's house was first searched for weapons and body wires. So, I was going in unarmed and that made me feel very naked and a bit vulnerable. I didn't feel much better when one of the narcotics detectives gave me a pack of cigarettes with an electronic device hidden inside of it. I asked him what it was for. He said, "You put it in your pocket. If you get shot and fall to the ground the device will send off an electronic signal that tells us you're in trouble." He asked me if I smoked. I told him that I didn't, but said that I would probably start as soon as I was done with this job.

For my ride, I was given a large four-wheel drive truck that looked like one of those monster trucks in beer commercials that drive over cars and crush them. The tires practically came up to my chest and I had a hard time climbing up to get inside of the cab. When it was finally time to go I said a prayer and the informant and I headed to the Snow Queen's palace. At the same time a legion of undercover cops were surrounding the perimeter of the house in unmarked vehicles and on foot.

The convict-snitch that was with me was as nervous as I was. He was sweating bullets and my adrenaline was through the roof. We drove down a long driveway and I parked near the front of the big house. Several other vehicles belonging to the bad guys were parked outside as well. Not long after the informant knocked on the front door, a hard-looking thug wearing a big handgun in a shoulder strap opened it and asked what we wanted. He didn't ask nicely either. Directly behind the first thug was another thug sitting in a chair just inside the door with some type of exotic automatic rifle leaning on the wall next to him. The informant told him that he was a friend of Ms. White's and needed to talk to her. The first thug eyed us for a moment and then had us step inside to an entryway and patted us both down. A third thug came out from a side room and led me to a dining room area while the informant was led down a hallway in the opposite direction. The thug that escorted me had a large Rambo-style knife on his belt and ordered me to sit down at a table near the kitchen.

I was now thinking that this whole wild plan wasn't such a good idea and that I was soon to be a dead man. At about that time I heard a woman yelling angrily down the hallway where the informant had been taken. My thug host sunk the tip of his big knife into the table directly in front of me and said with no uncertain terms, "Don't move," and he headed down the hallway.

I looked at the big knife stuck in the table for only a second. My feet didn't wait for me to make up my mind, they were on the way out of the house way ahead of me. I was happy to see the front entryway clear of thugs and surprised to see the informant outside sprinting in front of me already half way to the monster truck. It was a race.

As big and tall as that truck was, we didn't have any trouble getting up inside of it this time. Thankfully the truck started right up and with its big tires spinning fast, I left a 'lawn job' behind me that was second to none in the history of all lawn jobs. As we blasted away down the long driveway, heading for the main street, it looked like someone had thrown a rock at a hornets' nest behind us. From my rear view mirror I could see thugs pouring out the front door and running to their cars to chase us down. With my pedal to the metal we roared to safety and hid a distance away where we caught our breath before returning to the police department.

The police surveillance team, who had been keeping close-watch, never had to blow their cover. I suspect, like guardian angels, they interceded on the street between me and the bad guys so that the snitch and I could put some distance behind us.

The informant was returned to prison and given a deserved sentence reduction for the valiant attempt he had made. I am sure that the prosecutor gave consideration to the fact that the informant would probably never step foot back into the state since he now is a marked man. The Snow Queen somehow avoided the cops on this occasion, but went down soon after on a federal rap with the help of the A.T.F. (Alcohol, Tobacco, Firearms) agency.

Maybe I was an adrenaline junky or maybe I was a fool, but I volunteered for every dangerous mission that came my way. It was as if every opportunity was an exciting adventure. So many people today like to watch police and detective shows on television, the spicier the better. For me, reading about something or watching it on a flat screen doesn't quite satisfy my hunger for life, I have to live it.

THE REVEALING TRUTH

CHAPTER FOUR

I learned early in my police career that every crime that's committed leaves a clue. My job was to find that clue. I believe most cops are like treasure hunters, they will race to be the first to find the hidden clue. It is almost like a game, a serious game, but a game just the same. Yet, clues aren't always easy to find. They come in all sizes and forms. Some come in puzzles which makes the game even more exciting. Solving mysteries was always my most favorite game. Putting bad guys in jail was only the icing on the cake.

Crooks generally leave more clues as they are leaving a crime scene than they do when they are entering one. On the way in they are trying to be more careful and are thinking more clearly. But once they have broken inside a house or a business and gained entry their heart is racing, their adrenaline flowing, and they perspire uncontrollably. Adrenaline can be a detective's best friend. Adrenaline, coupled with fear, causes perspiration. Perspiring hands leave nice hand and fingerprints. Adrenaline also sometimes triggers one to naturally have the need to find a restroom quickly. Bad guys are physically no different than anyone else. They often find themselves having to desperately relieve themselves and sometimes actually do while they are in the middle of their criminal work. Bad guys are lazy people at heart and when they do use their victim's restroom they seldom flush the toilet. It's not a pleasant discovery for the police officer or detective who later investigates the crime scene, but it's potential D.N.A. evidence. When I investigated a crime such as a burglary, one of the first places I searched for evidence were the toilets.

If you want to be a good 'Treasure Hunter' you have to be willing to look for evidence in places that one wouldn't expect to find it. There is always a clue somewhere and the challenge for cops is to find it and solve the mystery.

It is always a bonus finding the case-breaking clue and then presenting it to the suspect who had thought he or she had committed the perfect crime. There is nothing better than seeing the expression on the criminal's face when you present their blunder to them. It is what cops live for.

A young single woman living in a downtown apartment was raped in the middle of the night by a stranger who had broken into her home. Shortly after the woman called 911, a suspect walking in the area was stopped and questioned by police. The man denied going in or near the apartments where the woman lived. The victim was unable to identify her offender because her room had been very dark, so the man that was stopped by police was released after he was questioned and identified.

These were the days before D.N.A. testing was available and so the Evidence Technician spent a great deal of time carefully looking for fingerprints and other small trace evidence. One of the items collected for fingerprint testing was a small cut-out paper doll that had been hanging on the victim's ceiling. It was one of many hanging on her walls and ceiling as decorations, but as destiny would have it, that one small paper doll fell onto the young woman's bed during the violent act. Miraculously, it had the evidence that contained the invisible proof; a fingerprint that linked the suspect to this horrible crime. This fingerprint belonged to the man who police had questioned and who had denied going near the apartment. He was soon apprehended and confessed to the crime. Another mystery solved, thanks to a determined Evidence Tech and a little paper angel who had miraculously floated down from a ceiling.

I was working an undercover detail in a downtown area when I saw a prostitute in a parking lot walk up to a couple of gentlemen sitting in a car nearby. The hopeful hooker flashed the two gents who were actually undercover cops that I was working with. We were working on a sting of some sort and had to rush the woman on her way so that we could get our attention back onto our job. Sadly, a few days later the woman was found dead, brutally murdered. A suspect was developed in the investigation and questioned, but he insisted that he did not harm the woman. The coroner, however, located some evidence that would prove his story not to be true.

When the prostitute was examined by the Coroner, he discovered what appeared to be bite marks on her neck. My partner and I, with a court order in hand, picked up the suspect who was being detained in jail and transported him to an oral surgeon who took an impression of his teeth. The suspect had a noticeable gap in his front two upper teeth. The Coroner had provided us with a jar that had a portion of the woman's neck inside so that the oral surgeon could compare the wound with the suspect's teeth. This was the evidence we were looking for, his gapped teeth and the bite mark were a match and the suspect was caught.

Unsolved mysteries are the ones that continue to haunt me. Like the summer where an unknown male suspect had broken into several apartments and had been raping single women who were living alone. The strikes were random and because of the many apartment complexes in the vicinity, stake-outs were difficult to cover.

The last reported strike occurred at an apartment where the woman wasn't touched by the suspect, but we knew it was our creep because the M.O. of entry was the same. The suspect went into apartments that were all located on the first floor, occupied by single women who were close to the same age.

The Evidence Technician determined that after the suspect had gotten inside the apartment and into the sleeping woman's bedroom, he removed certain garments from the woman's dresser. He took the garments back to her living room, opened a sofa-bed and proceeded to watch television with the woman's apparel on or around him. At some point, he went to the kitchen and picked up a large butcher knife and carried it back into the bedroom where the woman was still sleeping peacefully. When the woman woke up that morning to go to work, she found the big knife lying on the bed beside her face.

I watched the Evidence Technician work feverishly to find any evidence, and the final process used at the scene caused those of us watching to shudder. The Evidence Tech had sprayed a mist of a special fingerprint lifting agent on the outside of the apartment's sliding glass door and it revealed a full frontal body impression left by the suspect. The image clearly showed a large bearded man pressing his body and face against the glass door as he lifted it up off its tracks to gain entry. The facial image was contorted, but very visible. It was as though we were looking into the face of the devil himself. All the cops looking at this stared silently at the human print for some time in awe. It was then that the woman's fear became very real to all of us. In fact, the terror that had been so cruelly left with all of the victims became very clear to us.

The suspect was gone and to my knowledge never located.

Causing fear is a twisted element of rape that I don't understand. I can't conceive its need, desire, or pleasure. Criminals like this man were my inspiration to become a cop in the first place. As long as there is evil a good cop can never rest.

WHAT'S UP DOC?

CHAPTER FIVE

I started out as a reserve police officer for a mid-sized city and I rode with a veteran cop who was going to show me the ropes. One night we pulled over a drunk driver who was an older fellow driving a big boat of a car. While the veteran cop was dealing with the man, I could see that the man was so smashed he could barely walk or talk. His blood alcohol level turned out to be the highest the officer had ever processed. I believe it was a 4.2 which is deadly drunk.

Back at the police station I looked at the man's driver's license as it was sitting on top of a table in the DUI Processing Room. My eyes bulged out of my head when I realized the mumbling intoxicated man was my own dentist. I had gone to this dentist since I was a small child and I hadn't even recognized him. I was shocked. I couldn't believe that my nice, mild mannered, gentle dentist could be this bumbling man who couldn't even keep his bloodshot eyes open and who couldn't talk without slurring his words. I quickly left the room hoping he was too drunk to recognize me. While I was out of view trying to take this all in it hit me, I had an appointment with him only a day or two away. Fortunately for me, my dentist was truly a good man and a good dentist. At the appointment he never showed any signs that he remembered me from his terrible arrest situation and his hands were as steady and gentle as ever.

I did a lot of growing up during my first year learning about police work. There is a culture for every profession, a unique language, behavior, and thought process that develops over a period of time. In the Rookie stage, a new cop is excited and zealously ready to change the world.

After two or three years on the force, the cocky side comes out. The badge makes one feel immortal and a bit above the law and the rest of the world. Finally a good healthy knock-down-drag-out fight comes along and its good medicine. There is always someone out there who doesn't care you're a cop and wants the chance to toss you around a room.

After a few more years, cops become a bit calloused and the badge begins to lose its shine. You become discouraged when all the hard work you put into a case ends up with the suspect walking out of the courtroom with a not guilty verdict. You come to the realization that people really don't care that you're only human. It takes many hours working a case from start to finish, and many times cops must sacrifice their personal time spent with their families and friends during holidays and special occasion in order to help make our cities safer. Christmas can be a tough time for cops. They respond to many domestic violence calls and suicides around holidays where you would think people would be jollier. It's a lonely feeling too sitting in a patrol car listening to Bing Crosby on the radio while you know your family and friends are together without you enjoying a nice hot turkey dinner.

If a cop makes it past 10 years they have accomplished much. By this time veteran cops are quieter than their younger peers and have stopped telling their wives or husbands about all the crazy calls they responded to when they get home from work. They keep their experiences inside and try to digest them on their own. They don't trust police administration, they give up on prosecutors, they become bitter about the world and they isolate themselves from many of their own friends. Veteran cops die far too young. Many of them have experienced as much violence and heartache as any soldier on the front lines. I spent about 23 years on the frontlines, but somehow survived the war. I attribute this partly because I kept one foot in my work and the other with my family and friends who were not cops.

I was at my doctor's office recently and the nurse told me that she was dating a cop and wanted my advice. My advice probably wasn't what she was hoping to hear. I let her know that if I were her father I would tell her that the dumbest thing she could do would be to marry a cowboy, a cop, or a musician. I also let her know that it was a sin and that she could go to hell for even thinking about it. She didn't take me serious, but I am sure one day she will look back and remember the old wise man with the good advice who cried out in pain when she intentionally stuck him hard with the big needle.

THE MAN IN THE BALLROOM GOWN

CHAPTER SIX

One of the fun facts about being a cop is that you never know what to expect anytime and anywhere. I was working patrol in a residential area on the northwest side of town when I was dispatched to check on a mental health patient who had not been reporting in to his counselor. It was a nice day and the four-plex apartments were relatively quiet for the most part. After getting the man's name and apartment number from the dispatcher, I walked up to the door and knocked on it while instinctively standing off to the side. Cops are trained to do this because so many have been blown away by shotgun blasts from crooks on the other side waiting for them. As soon as I knocked on the door I heard a loud 'BANG' coming from close by. It wasn't a gunshot type of bang, but more of a 'somebody dropped a heavy anvil on top of a metal roof kind of bang.' I looked around trying to figure out where the noise was coming from, but there was nothing in sight. A few on-lookers who were standing around the area, however, disappeared back into their homes. I stood in my place believing that the noise was nothing important, but when I knocked on the door again, 'BANG' went the noise again. At this point I realized that the noise might be coming from the other side of the door. I was amused, so I knocked on the door again and 'BANG' it went even louder. I identified myself as a police officer, but didn't get a reply. Officer Jake Evans who had been in the area stopped by like a good back-up officer does and asked me what was going on. I said, "Hey, Jake, check this out," and I knocked on the door again. 'BANG' came the loud noise which sent Jake Evans back a couple of steps. Jake and I looked at each other with big smiles. "Cool."

I told Jake why I was there and had him watch the front door, which was the only door to the residence, and I went around to the side of the apartment to try to peak through a window. There was one just around the corner from the front door that had a broken blind that was separated wide enough for me to look inside the apartment. I carefully put my face up to the window (this was a dumb and dangerous move) where I barely was able to see inside.

At first I wasn't sure if what I was seeing was real, but as my eyes adjusted to the darkened interior I began making out the scene. There was just enough light coming from the closed blinds of the apartment's window to see heaps of furniture lying on the floor smashed into pieces. A shattered coffee table, a dining room table broken to bits, busted chairs, broken glass, smashed pictures, all throughout the living room and dining area.

While I was trying to make out the disaster, my back-up Officer Jake Evans knocked on the front door and loudly announced who he was. I would have never expected what happened immediately afterwards. Out from a back room and into a hallway came a shadowy figure walking in my direction. As the dark figure came into the living room and into better lighting, there revealed a mind-blowing image of a man in his 40's, about 6 foot, unshaven and unkempt, and wearing a beautiful blue sequin, full length, ballroom gown. Now this, in the liberal city where I worked might not be all that unusual since it is a very diverse community, but what caught my attention was the large single edged axe that the spooky man held in front of him.

He looked like one of those wooden figures that pop out of a coo-coo clock at the top of the hour. But this 'coo-coo' swung the axe into the door that Officer Evans was just on the other side of.

So that was what the big banging noise was all about! I poked my head back around the corner to see my officer friend still looking bewildered. When I told Jake what I had just witnessed inside, his curiosity changed to more of a survival mode and he pulled out his handgun.

Eventually more troops were rounded up and it was decided we needed to go in and help the man who obviously was having some mental problems.

Police officers have an unwritten code called, 'You catch 'em, you clean 'em,' so I was the front-man to go inside. The 'You catch 'em, you clean 'em' code, is a universal police procedure and has its rewards, but it also has its drawbacks. The first officer on any scene is generally made the 'primary officer.' The primary officer is the one who gets stuck writing the bulk of the reports and transporting the crooks to jail and all those other boring details that keeps one off the streets. The street is where the action is, not the patrol room or the jail. Being first officer on the scene can be extremely exhilarating. You get to be shot at first, you get hands on the bad guys first and all that fun stuff. But if you got to 'clean 'em' it isn't all that exciting.

Officer Evans and Officer Wes Vernon were behind me, and after a quick huddle, the apartment manager unlocked the front door and let us in. We went in single file. I was in a crouching position with a semi-automatic handgun pointed in front of me. Officer Evans was directly behind me and standing just above me with his handgun held in an outstretched hand keeping watch on our sides while Officer Vernon, the number three man, with weapon ready, secured the rear. The patrol sergeant that responded, like all smart veterans, kept a distance away and stayed outside.

Once inside the living room, I holstered my handgun and picked up a long piece of broken wood that had come from one of the shattered furniture items inside. I felt safer with the piece of wood than I did my handgun, because I knew that simply unloading a magazine of bullets into a determined man didn't guarantee stopping him. I figured I could use the wood like a jousting pole and at least keep the man at a distance if he charged.

Holding our breath we went around each corner and methodically checked each destroyed room. We found the poor man quietly sitting in his bedroom closet. It was clear by looking at the amount of debris and the terrible odor surrounding us, that he had been living in his closet for quite some time. We brought him safely out without any problem.

Folks with mental illness were always a special lot to me. I learned over time and experience that many people grow up very normal and happy and then one day they slip away into sad, difficult, and chaotic lives sometimes never mentally coming back. I never understood why some people, and even some cops, could look down their noses at someone as unfortunate as that poor man in the blue ballroom gown.

Officer Evans and Officer Vernon were good cops, compassionate, resourceful and I liked working with them. We were able to work the Foot Patrol downtown together not too long after this incident. During that time we helped many of the mentally ill who roamed the streets trying to find their way back.

DEAD MEN *DO* TELL TALES

CHAPTER SEVEN

It was the coldest winter that I could ever remember and it snowed that year. My new partner, Officer Hansen, had just moved up from southern California where he had been an officer and had not been in the snow before. Our job was to patrol the downtown area of the city on foot. Hansen could barely move with the several layers of long-johns he was wearing beneath his winter uniform. He looked like the gingerbread man walking down the road with an Elmer Fudd winter hat that made him look even sillier. The snow was deep and we spent some time helping street kids push a giant ball of snow in a downtown park to make a big snowman. The snowball got so big we had to abandon it in the middle of an intersection because we couldn't push the heavy thing any further. We high-tailed it out of the area before someone called 911.

That same cold winter, I believe it was February and it was around 1:00 a.m. when I was dispatched to a house in a nice quiet neighborhood. An elderly woman needed help finding her husband and she wanted assistance because she had poor eye sight. When I arrived, the woman was frantic and latched onto me like a piece of sticky saran wrap. She had to be in her eighties and was as round as she was tall. She wore thick glasses that made her eyes look huge, and she still couldn't see much farther than the nose on her face.

The upset woman told me that she had been talking on her telephone and when she finished the call she realized her husband was gone. She had called his name many times but he didn't answer. She feared that he had died somewhere in the house. To make matters worse, her husband had been experiencing flu-like symptoms and had a recent medical history with his ticker that was going to require an operation. The scenario she gave didn't sound good, so I prepared my mind for an unpleasant find.

I told the woman that I would check her house for her. She insisted she go with me, so she hooked her arm around mine and pulled me close causing me to practically drag her throughout the house. We went from room to room without finding her missing husband. With each empty room the woman's stress level and the volume of her concerned voice grew to the point I was worried she would have her own heart failure. Occasionally she would have to sit down to catch her breath, but she still insisted that she hold onto my arm while I continue the search.

I asked the woman every question I could think of to solve the mystery. "Could he have gone to visit a neighbor?" "How long has he been gone?" "Could a relative or friend have picked him up?" The woman was certain that her husband was in the house when she was on the phone and that he would not be at a neighbor's house. She added that all of their relatives lived out of state. The only other place he might be, she recalled, was in a little workshop outside.

Again, it was one o'clock in the morning. This was all so very strange and I started to wonder if the woman might not be simply having a 'moment.'

With the sweet hysterical lady stuck to my side, we went into her backyard to search the workshop for her missing husband. It was so cold outside that the grass was frozen and covered with white frost and my ears immediately felt the stinging from a blast of frozen February wind.

The door on the shop was locked from the outside, so it was obvious that the woman's husband wasn't inside the shop. There were no footprints on the grass, so he hadn't passed through the yard. The night was as quiet and still as a country graveyard.

Then I saw it. An older model sedan parked under an attached carport at the end of a concrete walkway. It was the kind of car that maybe an old missing man would drive. The elderly woman must have sensed my concern because she tensed up and squeezed tighter onto my arm and pressed up closer. I asked her to go inside while I checked the car and she adamantly refused. I asked her to remain where she was so that I could check the car and with a squealing, "Don't leave me here," confirmation made it very clear that she was going with me while I checked inside the car.

Her fear and reluctance to go to the car made the short walk feel like I was dragging a big anchor, but I finally reached the driver's door to look inside. The windows were frosted up, but I was able to see what I suspected. It appeared that the woman's husband had been sitting in the driver's seat when he probably suffered a heart attack. At some point, he rolled over onto his back and died. Both of his hands were curled up at his chest with their twisted old colorless fingers contorted and frozen, either by death or by the cold weather. His face was a pale blue-gray color and his eyes and mouth were partly open and still. It appeared as though he had been dead for some time.

I didn't say anything and began to draw back from the car to get the woman back inside the house before she dropped dead herself. She could tell by my silence that something was terribly wrong and she cried out, "He's in there isn't he?" I didn't answer and said that we needed to get back into the house. She didn't budge. Again she cried out, "He's in there!" nearly ripping my arm off. I then told her that her husband was indeed in the car. She hit the roof. "He's dead isn't he?" she screeched. I didn't answer which wasn't the answer she wanted from me. After wrestling with her a moment I finally gave in, "Yes, he's gone." This statement was followed by a wail that I will never forget. Decades of marriage, love, companionship was over, finished, kaput, done, the end.

The sad old woman finally surrendered to herself in a lump of tears and I helped her back into the house giving as much empathy as I could muster. "Are you sure there isn't someone I can call to help you through this?" I asked. "No, they're all living out of state," she sobbed. "Do you have a minister or someone from your faith I can call?" I offered. "No, there's no one." she sobbed helplessly.

The woman went immediately to her telephone and began calling every one of her grown up children to report the bad news. "Your dad is dead," she told her attorney son in San Francisco tearfully. I heard her give the bad news to another son, a physician in Phoenix, another child in another part of the country and so on. All the while she was on the phone there was something nagging at me to get back to the body in the car. However, the new widow refused to let me out of her sight so I stayed by her side, contacted the police dispatcher on my radio and waited for the coroner.

It didn't take long for my first line supervisor, Corporal Smith, to stop by for the low-down.

Sgt. Taylor also stopped by to help console the upset woman who was still on the telephone crying and spreading the sad news of her dead husband to every living relative she had.

And it wasn't long after the police dispatcher announced that the coroner was on the way that my short career flashed before my eyes. The old woman was on the phone making death notifications to her relatives, I was explaining what had transpired to Sgt. Taylor, and Cpl. Smith was just about to go out the back door to check on the deceased when suddenly the dead man walked into the room. The old man didn't make a sound and simply smiled as if he was happy to have company over. Other than appearing very old and still having a bluish-gray skin color, the old-timer looked like he was ready to go 18 holes on a golf course.

I guess I was in shock because the first thing that came out of my mouth was a loud and squeaky, "You're supposed to be dead!" The old man only shrugged his shoulders and quietly sat down and said nothing. His wife bellowed even louder and I am not certain what, if any, words were coming out of her mouth, but she wasn't a happy woman. I could only think of all the calls she had just made to her children and relatives and wondered how I would explain my blunder to anyone.

Cpl. Smith was a former Marine sniper who had seen and done it all. He looked over at me and gave a callus raise of his eye brows and said, "Guess I'm not needed here, see ya later," and headed back out to his patrol car. Sgt. Taylor, on the other hand, like me, was an adventurer and enjoyed the wild surprises of the job. He was one of those 'cup is half full' people who view getting fired as an opportunity for new adventures. He slipped in a big smile and let me know how much fun the adventure was going to be when the boss, Chief Wilson, read my report in the morning.

It turned out that the old man had grown tired of his wife always talking on the telephone and decided to give her a scare. I don't know how long he waited for her out in his cold car and I don't know if he realized she had called the cops to help her, but I do know that he gave me the scare of my life. The chewing out speech I received from Chief Wilson nearly peeled my paint.

The mayor of the city, as well as the city manager, the chief of police, and of course yours truly would be named in a lawsuit by the angry professional children of the dead man who wasn't dead, but should have been dead and at least looked dead to me. Now *I* was the dead man. Fortunately for me, however, the nice elderly woman's not-so-dead husband talked their children out of coming down on me and the city, saying that I was a nice young man with the best of intentions.

Chief Wilson never said another word about it. Other than being called a 'Miracle Healer' by my peers for several years, the only repercussions I have is that this story is still told in basic law enforcement academies, to this day, for the purpose of death investigation training...'What not to do.' I couldn't be happier to have it all behind me.

THE MISSING KEY MYSTERY

CHAPTER EIGHT

It was a slow night in the city and Diane was the lone receptionist at a popular four-star high rise motel near the waterfront. A traveling business woman who was staying alone in an upper room had been assaulted by an unknown male intruder that had somehow entered her locked room in the middle of the night. Many officers raced to the call, set up a perimeter, and searched for the suspect, but couldn't find the bad guy or any leads to his whereabouts.

A detective was called out and interviewed the victim who said that she was certain she locked the door when she went to bed. There were no signs of forced entry on the door. The detective then began to intensely interview Diane the receptionist. Diane told him that there were only two ways to get a key to any of the rooms. She would give one to the customer and the extra keys were kept on a wall directly behind her to keep them out of reach from anyone coming into the lobby. There were no other employees in the building and no one had come into or out of the hotel during the time frame of the crime. The detective was mystified and may have even wondered if the victim was telling the truth.

It had been at least an hour since the assault, and all but one of the patrol officers had gone back to doing their routine patrol work. Officer Callahan remained and cruised up and down the city blocks in his patrol car hoping he could spot anyone out of place. I was on Foot Patrol, so I remained in the vicinity snooping around for clues.

Something nagged at my gut and I wanted badly to solve this mystery, so I put on my thinking cap. As corny as this may sound, I had a ritual that I performed at most every major crime that I investigated. This consisted of simply stopping in my tracks, listening for any sounds that were out of place, and asking the crime scene (the hotel and surrounding area) to reveal to me its clues. I walked slowly out a back door of the hotel into a covered parking garage and then out into an alley that went alongside the hotel. I continued very slowly, carefully listening, and waiting for the answers. And then I saw it! A small drain pipe coming from the parking garage and spilling onto the alley's surface emitted a little light at the end of it. I bent down and looked into the pipe to see the silhouette of an object that seemed out of place. I fixed my flashlight on the object in the pipe. It was a key! It was a hotel key that bore the same number of the woman's room.

The key's discovery prompted the receptionist to spill the beans. She told the detective that while she was working behind the reception desk she desperately needed to use the restroom which was located behind the lobby desk. A daytime cook happened to stop by and she asked him to watch the front counter for a couple of minutes while she freshened up. When she returned to her post, the cook was gone and she never noticed the missing key.

The truth was revealed, the cook's goose was cooked and he was quickly located and gave a full confession. Sometimes the key to solving a mystery is a key itself. Every crime can be solved if you simply search for the key.

NOBODY'S FALL GUY

CHAPTER NINE

There were many times that I drove with my lights totally blacked out when I was on night patrol. While the good citizens were sleeping peacefully in their beds, I would roll my patrol car windows down, keep my police radio volume low, turn off all my lights, and drive slowly through alleys and neighborhoods for hours. I listened intently for any sound; a window breaking, a dog barking, a burglar or thief whispering to their accomplice, anything. I'd hide in the shadows and sit with my motor off just waiting, watching and hoping for something to move. Crime moves, and at night anything that moves is suspect.

It's amazing how much you can hear at night when you are quiet and listening. Even the smart crooks know this. They can hear a cop car's radio and cruiser patrolling the streets from many blocks away, and they almost always know where the cop cars are if they're moving. Thus, it's a rare moment to catch smart crooks by surprise while their fingers are in someone's cookie jar.

We'd been getting hit hard with car prowlers in my district for quite a while. This was making me and the officers assigned to that district look bad. It was late at night and I told another officer that I was going out prowling myself to finally catch 'em' red handed.

It was St. Patty's Day and there was still a little life left in the taverns. I went straight to a string of businesses located off a main road in my district and turned onto a side road and shut off my lights, rolled down my windows, and turned my radios down to where I could barely hear the police chatter. I then drove slowly behind a restaurant and looked over toward the tavern and noticed someone in the dark moving behind a truck. I stopped quickly and let my eyes adjust to the darkness. Other than a bit of light coming from the back door of the tavern, everything was pitch-black. I waited for a few moments and when I didn't see any more movement, I decided I would surprise the person by pulling up quickly to the back parking lot of the tavern with my lights off and then when I got in position I would turn on every light I had.

Good city police cars have plenty of lights. Other than the obvious headlights, there are hand controlled spotlights at the door-posts. There are also two powerful flood lights on each side of the roof's light bar and even more powerful 'Take-Down Lights' at the front of the light bar. Utilizing all of these lights at the same time is pretty impressive to say the least.

The back parking lot of the tavern was gravel and was set back from the tavern. There was a fence with a hedge to my left that blocked the entire view of the rear of the parking lot and at first I didn't see that there was an occupied car hidden in the shadows.

As soon as I entered the parking lot and got into position, I lit every light on my patrol car simultaneously. It was then that I saw the car in the rear lot that had been hiding in the shadows. The mystery car was facing toward the tavern and had two occupants. The two were sitting close together in the front seat of the car. I figured they were just a couple of romantics and not what I'd hoped for. At almost the same moment, I saw one of the locals zipping up his pants on the other side of the truck and realized what I had seen was just a drunk ridding some of his daily habit. I shut my lights back down and parked my car.

Disappointed at my find, I warned the drunk to be more mindful where he relieved himself. I hoped to save some professionalism and decided to go over to the car and tell the lovers why I had made such a grand appearance.

The two romantics were now at opposite ends of the front bench seat of the car. As I came closer with my flashlight aimed to the ground, I realized I recognized the man who was now cowered down low in his seat almost hugging the door. He was a very well known, high ranking political figure. The pretty young woman with him was in her early twenties and was now leaning against the opposite door looking a bit blushed. She didn't say a word, but her face said a thousand words. A mobile phone was sitting on the dashboard providing just enough light to see that the female was wearing a business-style top and skirt.

The political figure sat so low in his seat that he had to almost gaze straight up at me when I approached him. My 'fight or flight juice' kicked in a bit, but I did a good job pretending I didn't know who he was or what I had just seen. I told the two that this area had been getting hit heavy by car prowlers and asked them if they had seen what the man by the truck was up to. The politician also had his 'fight or flight juice' in control. He told me they hadn't noticed the man and that they were just out in the car talking because the bar was either too hot or too smoky, something to that effect.

I thanked them and told them to have a good night as I walked back to my patrol car with my eyes bulging and jaw hanging open. I hadn't even made it to my car when I heard the politician's car engine rev up and gravel flying as it sped away out of the back parking lot racing back towards the city's downtown area.

While the politician and his friend sped away, another officer drove into the lot from the opposite side, and I excitedly told him who I had just encountered and how it came about. Lieutenant Meadows was the on-duty shift supervisor, so I immediately told him exactly what had happened. Lt. Meadows smoked a pipe and liked to fly fish. He was quiet, even keeled, and a man of great wisdom. Well, I'm not totally sure about the wisdom part, but I do know he smoked a pipe and liked to fly fish, so I figured he was someone I could trust.

Lt. Meadows smiled and told me not to tell a soul about what had happened. He instructed me to write a detailed letter to the chief of police, not a report, but a confidential letter and he would give the letter directly to the chief. "As you know, John, the chief doesn't like surprises and you never know where this might go," Lt. Meadows wisely told me. Boy, was he ever right.

I did my part and kept the story to myself. I don't suppose it was more than a couple of days later when every radio personality, every television and newspaper reporter in the state, and at least one reporter nationally wanted to know what Officer Weber had seen behind the tavern on St Patty's Day. The stories were out of this world, even obscene and illegal, many of them. I heard one of the popular hot-talk radio hosts begging me on the air to call him and give him the scoop. Media trucks with their transmission dishes high in the air on cranes set up camp for a time around city hall hoping Chief Williams would be forced to give them the breaking story. Chief Williams was another adventurer though, and he delighted in holding out and keeping them wondering. The media is never a cop's friend and Chief Williams wasn't about to give them any satisfaction.

The officer that showed up at the tavern parking lot, Lt. Meadows, and the chief of police were the only ones I told, so I have no clue how the story ever manifested itself and was disclosed to the public. But then again, there are some bad odors in this world that just can't be hidden.

The wild rumors and crazy stories continued their course. No doubt, political explanations were being demanded from the other side of the aisle. Those explanations were apparently demanded from the politician's wife as well.

One day Chief Williams called me into his office and told me that the politician's 'people' wanted to interview me. They actually wanted me to be sworn in at the State's Supreme Court to give a statement under oath of what had occurred. My chief said that he had been informed that the politician's wife was very upset about the rumors of her husband being with another woman, and it was causing problems at home. I confidently told Chief Williams that I would be happy to. He smiled at my answer.

It was like a game of poker. The politician was a desperate liar and having me testify under oath was obviously a failed bluff. He never faced me head on, but sent several three piece suits to a big important secret meeting between 'his people' and 'my people.'

It took place in City Hall behind closed doors. On behalf of my police department was yours truly, the city manager, city attorney, Chief Williams, and a few other police administrators wearing brass on their collars. On behalf of the politician were some very important looking men in nice suits and shiny shoes, and also included was the politician's Press Secretary, and a middle-aged woman who looked very plain and who kept very quiet.

Chief Williams asked me to tell everyone in the room what had transpired on the past St Patty's Day behind the tavern. I was asked many questions by the Press Secretary who would have made a great police detective. She told me that the politician admitted that he was the one that I had contacted behind the tavern, but the woman was a friend of his family and that they were simply talking with each other because the woman was having problems at home.

"Would you recognize the woman you saw with (politician) if you saw her again?" the Press Secretary asked.

"Yes," I quickly replied.

The Press Secretary pointed to the plain looking, quiet woman sitting twenty feet away from me and asked, "What would you say, if I was to tell you that the woman you saw with (politician), is that woman sitting over there?" The Press Secretary went on to say that the woman was wearing the same clothes that she had on the night that I contacted the politician in the parking lot.

Not so! The woman I had seen with the politician was about 22 years old, pretty, long dark hair, with some type of origin that gave her a light brown skin color. She didn't have short graying hair; she wasn't frumpy, wearing a blue sweatshirt with Alaska or something like that written on the front of it.

It was at that point my milk began to curdle and my hospitable smile vanished. The politician was going to try to use me as his fall guy for his evil deed. He apparently didn't know his opponent's history very well.

I shot back, "*She* is not the woman *I* saw with (politician)."

"Would you be willing to swear to that in a court room?" the Press Secretary challenged.

"Yes, I would," I replied confidently.

Chief Williams had been waiting for this moment. He had a big grin on his face. "John, how old do you think that woman is?" the chief asked, referring to the fake.

After studying the woman a moment, I replied and gave my best estimate, "Around forty-two."

The Press Secretary asked the woman how old she was and with a solemn expression on her face and lowering her eyes the frumpy woman mumbled, "Forty-two."

Chief Williams beamed. The meeting was over. The Press Secretary looked furious and not too long after this incident she resigned. The event had stirred up plenty of other trouble for the politician who eventually left office. It wasn't over for me, though, life then began to get a bit more bizarre.

Sometimes who you know can be beneficial, but sometimes who you know can be a deficit...once upon a time there was a politician who I wished I had never met.

PRANK GONE BAD

CHAPTER TEN

'0-Dark Thirty' for cops is when the town rolls up and the radio stops cracking. In my city that was usually about 4:00 a.m. It's at that time the 'Sleep Monster' starts creeping up behind you. If you didn't have a lot of paperwork, then you'd better stay busy doing something or you'd have a hard time staying awake until the end of your shift at 7:00 a.m.

Officer Mel Rourke was a good cop. He was a patrol officer and knew his beat better than any other cop around. Rourke usually worked nights and after the calls slowed down he would keep busy by 'prowling' his patrol cruiser through alleys and on the streets looking for vehicle prowlers, burglars, and anyone that might be out looking for a reason to go to jail.

Rourke knew every old pry mark made by a burglar's tool on every business in his district. He would get out of his patrol car, look for any new pry marks, and shake doors to make sure they were secured. He was a pretty handy guy to have around and made an excellent resource for knowing who the bad boys were.

At the time my partner, Wes Vernon, and I were assigned to the downtown bicycle unit. Imagine riding a police mountain bike all year round and getting paid for it, now that is living. We could move around quickly and silently. Heavy traffic during the daytime wasn't a problem for us and we could beat any patrol car or ambulance to any urgent call. At night we were stealth crime fighters.

One night we watched Officer Rourke drive into a part of our district. We figured that Rourke must have finally gotten bored in his own district and came down to poach for bad guys in ours. We followed his patrol car from a distance as he 'slow-rolled' through an industrial area on the north edge of town.

Some motorist must have made a wrong turn somewhere and ended up getting stopped by Officer Rourke. A light bulb suddenly went off in my head. I signaled for Officer Vernon to stop with me in a dark area and asked him to hold onto my bike while I tried to sneak up on Rourke and hide in his patrol car. Officer Vernon smiled, possibly because he thought it was a great idea, or possibly because it was his opportunity to see me finally get in trouble without him.

While Officer Rourke was busy talking to the stopped motorist, I silently rushed up and slipped into the back seat of his cruiser and then quietly closed the door behind me. As I hunkered down out of sight I practically had a hernia trying to contain myself from laughing out loud.

Officer Rourke returned to his patrol car, got in, and then before long we were off. I don't know what my partner was thinking back there, but I hoped he was having as much fun as I was. I kept quiet and didn't move a muscle for about 10 minutes. Officer Rourke proceeded to slowly patrol my district as he happily hummed some 80's pop song to himself.

The industrial area at night can be sort of spooky if you're working alone, or at least think you're alone. It's grey, remote, and full of shadows, sort of like an old Mickey Spillane mystery novel. Only a few street lights went by as we cruised around the empty streets. Finally, I decided to make my move. I knew that there was a street light coming up, and just at the right time I slowly sat up. It was perfect timing for my move because there was just enough light from the street lamp to throw a thin line of light across my eyes. Officer Rourke's eyes and mine met in his rear view mirror at that magical moment and the response I got was more than I expected.

Officer Rourke was a full grown man with a fairly deep voice, but I swear the man sounded like a frightened schoolgirl falling off a roller coaster. His blood curdling scream started at a high decibel pitch with incredible volume. But then, as he recognized the grinning chump in the back seat of his car, his voice curled back down to a low growling devious chuckle. I knew I was in trouble because the chuckle went on for a long time. And more importantly, I'd forgotten that once you get in the back seat of a patrol car, there is only one way out. That, of course, is by the willing cop on the outside.

I think my partner, Officer Vernon, knew my fate from the beginning and was somewhere laughing his lips off, while I spent the next two hours trapped in the back of Officer Rourke's patrol car. Officer Rourke even went as far as going to the police department to take a break and get a cup of coffee while keeping me prisoner in his back seat.

Leave it to Officer Rourke to stay awake after 0-Dark Thirty. If you can't beat the Sleep Monster, just keep him penned up in the back of your patrol car until it's time to go home.

GANGLAND IN THE HOMETOWN

CHAPTER ELEVEN

It was the years of reading graffiti from the streets of downtown that helped to keep me informed. Graffiti is the daily newspaper on the streets. My city's downtown was really *down* town. It's at the bottom between two hills and I always thought of it as the bottom of the world where all the scum settled. Some would say it is a very diverse, multi-cultural community, but in truth, it's a shady, seedy, greasy, and fairly dangerous place at night. It was the perfect fun place for an adventurous cop to work.

The police dispatchers use to call me, 'Down Town Johnny,' and were happy to work my shifts with me. Magic happened when I called in 10-8 (In Service). And although that magic wasn't always good for me, at least it was something to keep the dispatchers awake.

The downtown certainly was a melting pot of personalities. I saw the punk rockers come and go and come back again. Then there were metal heads, rockers, satanists, hippies, politicians, good college students, naughty ones, yuppies, drunk sailors from every part of the world, grunge rockers, skaters, gothies, war protesters, celebrities, folks from every sexual interest looking for love, bible thumpers, bikers, transients, cross dressers, mentally ill folks, street kids, drug dealers, and more. It was a kick. And then one day the street gangs showed up in town.

We already had Asian gang members living in a section of my town, however, they generally kept low key and went to other cities to do their evil deeds. It's sort of like that old saying that a dog always prefers to go potty in the neighbor's yard. I personally think that's just plain good manners.

Asian gangsters were always better at keeping their secrets than those in white or black street gangs. Some say that this is because prior to coming to America, their countries had been at war for so long that they had already learned the ropes of surviving in a violent world. They were better at keeping their lives and lies in order. I had done a lot of work helping South East Asian families and earned some trust and respect from that community. I suspect that this interaction was the blessing that kept me alive on a few occasions.

The 'XIV Gang' was a South East Asian 'Blood' street gang that was started by the children of first generation 'Boat People' who had fled from the Viet Nam War to the United States back in the 1970's. They were from places like Cambodia, Viet Nam, Laos, and were mostly good folks trying to survive. Unfortunately, many of their children were thrown into certain California neighborhoods that were already infested with black, white, and Hispanic street gangs, and sadly, some adapted to the violent American culture.

Gangs like the XIV were true survivalists. Trusting any American was understandably difficult for them. They rarely got caught and used a variety of weapons hidden close by in case of trouble with other gangs or in case of trouble with cops. At the time, the XIV connected themselves to the powerful 'Blood' gang which actually was a black gang that originated in Compton, California. The original 'Blood' gang consisted of Afro-Americans however over a period of time and growth they allowed some Asian street gangs like the XIV to affiliate in their criminal causes.

Blood gangs wore red colors, while the opposing Crip gangsters from southeast Los Angeles favored the color blue as they do to this day.

Gaining territory is important to all street gangs because it means more money from drug sales, extortion of businesses and recruiting membership. A larger city located a few miles north of the town that I worked in was infested with Crip gangs and the trouble they made had became so bad that it had paralyzed that entire city. Naturally, those Crip gangs began their quest to take over my town. That didn't go well with the local Asian Blood gangsters who enjoyed their peaceful safe-place in their hometown. It didn't go well with the police officers in my area either. These were tense times.

One night while I was on Foot Patrol, I ran into about a dozen XIV members who were hanging out by a public building in my district. They had been playing basketball at the community center and not bothering anyone. We joked around for a bit and then I went on my way. About a block away I saw a known Crip gangster standing inside a telephone booth. His street name was

'Tigger,' and he was a bad egg out of his sandbox. I suspected something was in the mix, so I went back to the XIV members and pretended to scold them for letting a Crip come into their territory. I then walked in the opposite direction with a smile on my face.

My partner, Officer Wes Vernon, and I had not been able to get the local politicians and some of the school officials to believe we had a serious growing gang problem, so I thought it best to let it take care of itself. It wasn't five minutes after walking away from the XIV members, my radio cracked, "Attention downtown units, citizen report of a black male being chased by a group of men yielding sticks." Tigger was a big healthy guy and I think he was able to outrun his shorter legged adversaries. He wasn't able to outrun his luck however. Sometime later he was given a life sentence for murder and now, once again, he's in someone else's territory.

Some people would think it was cold hearted to put a young man in such danger. Tigger wasn't innocently visiting the downtown area. He was up to something. He was a seasoned gangster and had been involved in many assaults, and probably homicide, so I wasn't terribly concerned if he got his lunch handed to him by the Asian gangsters.

I once heard a judge sentence a young man to a long prison sentence for a robbery downtown. He was a local street thug and one night he had tried to assault and rob a good citizen who had come downtown to meet friends for dinner. The thug was seriously injured by the citizen who fought back. While in court the thug complained that the citizen was uninjured, yet he had to go to the hospital. The judge had no pity for the street thug and told him, "If you are going to live on the streets, then you can live by the law of the streets." In other words, street justice is not a fair justice.

Life is rarely fair. I've seen too many unfortunate endings that would make me believe it's true.

Young Chad was an unfortunate ending. He was a rolly-polly kid who I coached in youth football. He was shy, likeable, and sort of quiet compared to the other boys. After football I lost track of him, but then one sad day several years later, I had to arrest him for murder.

A Crip gang from a larger city had managed to grow roots on the eastside of my city (the XIV was on the west side), and their strength was growing fast. Gang leaders, or 'O.G.s' were sending their urban gangsters to traffic dope and guns with the rural 'Tweekers' (methamphetamine users and manufacturers). This was one of the oddest mixes of culture that I had ever witnessed, big city black street gangs doing business with white red necks. The quest for making money has no pride.

During one illegal escapade, a group of these Crips were caught with their claws in a cookie jar. The youngest was a 17 year old named Lance who had been given a deal by the prosecutor to snitch on his partners and friends in crime. Lance's deal was that if he truthfully testified at trial, his involvement would be kept safe and confidential, so that he could join the Marines and get out of town when he turned 18. But, Lance and the prosecutor's office underestimated Lance's so-called friends.

The two Crip leaders who led their gang's efforts in my area were sly and devious and surrounded themselves with loyal and beautiful girlfriends and plenty of cash. Their pretty girlfriends were cold and covert and sometimes even more devious than they were. They rode with other gangsters who stabbed an innocent kid to death who had simply been walking down the street. The kid just happened to be wearing something with the color red, which was the Crip gangster's enemy flag.

Chad and Lance grew up together and were close friends. But according to Chad, one of the Crip gang leaders offered to give him his car to kill Lance. This would assure that Lance could not testify against the gang in the upcoming trial. The car was just a piece of garbage Monte Carlo, but for some reason Chad thought it was a good deal. Imagine, killing your long time friend for a three hundred dollar car.

Lance pretended that he didn't know anything about the prosecutor's offer and tried to convince his 'homies' that he would stand by them when it came time to go to trial. The Crip gang leaders knew better, thanks to an attorney that managed to learn about the offer. Regardless, Lance kicked around with his homies, all the while walking on dangerously thin ice.

Chad later told me that he brought a gang provided 9mm semi-automatic handgun to a large house party that Lance was invited to. At some point, as was planned, one of the Crip gangsters would turn off the house lights so Chad could shoot Lance without being seen. However, when it was time to pull the trigger Chad got cold feet.

The gang leaders continued to put pressure on Chad, but were getting nervous that maybe they had picked the wrong man for the job.

One night when Lance was visiting the gang's apartment, Chad talked Lance into giving him a ride home. Lance was reluctant because he was very aware that the trial was getting close. He also had high suspicions that one of his so-called-friends would try to kill him and that Chad was sketchy enough to do it. Yet, Lance did give Chad a ride and on the way, according to Chad, Lance pulled into an apartment complex to sell come Crack cocaine. Chad told Lance to stop the car at the entrance, and when he did, Chad began shooting Lance at close range. Chad, covered with the spray back of Lance's blood, continued shooting as he jumped out of the car. With the motor running and headlights still on, Lance slumped over the stirring wheel and was dead.

The plan was that one of the gang leaders would use his girlfriend's car to pick Chad up by a restaurant after the job was done. Chad slipped through the night and made it to a phone booth by a main road about 5 blocks away. Chad had cash in his wallet but no loose coins. Still covered in blood, he asked a couple of teens on skateboards for some change so that he could make his phone call. The gang leader never answered Chad's page, so Chad, like any other wholesome young man, decided to walk over to the restaurant to get something to eat. He was hungry. Such is the life of a gangster.

Our gang task force had a good idea that Chad was the gunman. The world is full of snitches and when Chad's name came up it was no surprise. He had been displaying outrageous behavior for several days prior to the murder. I suppose he was acting out because he was trying to build up his courage so that he could shoot his friend in the head. It's hard to say though, maybe he was acting like a big bad gangster because deep inside he was afraid. Peer pressure is stressful and very real.

Chad wasn't easy to find, but he did finally turn himself in and gave me a full confession. Unfortunately for the justice system, witnesses, victims, and suspects don't do very well on the witness stand in court hearings or trials when gangs are involved. The truth of 'Dead Men Tell No Tales' is alive and powerful in gangland. Each court hearing was filled with Crip gang members staring down every witness that came to give his or her testimony. Witnesses that went in strong and ready to tell the truth, shut their mouth, changed their story, or suddenly didn't know a thing. Chad obviously didn't fear death. He told it like it was without showing any emotion. The only evidence of remorse he ever displayed was not getting the three hundred dollar car that the gang leader had promised him.

There was some payback for one of the gang leaders, however, while being held in custody for the trial, his girlfriend spent many thousands of his dollars on clothes, a Caribbean Cruise, and other fine items and then ran off with some other gangster. Eventually the main gang leader who contracted the murder found his way to prison for life for other business deals gone bad.

It truly breaks my heart to think about that cute little rolly-polly shy kid on the football field who became so cold that he would kill one of his friends for a three hundred dollar car. This is a world I will never understand.

TWO JOKERS PER DECK

CHAPTER TWELVE

Officer Wes Vernon and I should have never been assigned the same shift. We certainly should not have been assigned to work as partners. We enjoyed life a little too much and we had a ball supplying the rest of the troops with surprises. It was like mixing two chemical components together that were destined for trouble. The trouble was usually harmless and often backfired.

Lt. Ford had his hands full when he was assigned to supervise the Foot Patrol where Wes and I worked and played. The downtown area was ours. We were like two kids with a sweet tooth in a candy store.

Lt. Ford did his best to control us and Wes and I did our best to be controlled. But how do you tame two Jackals in the wild world of fun? Nearly every day we got called into the office because of some pathetic citizen complaint. Tying a sleeping drunk's boot strings together, play wrestling with street kids, talking smack to snobby citizens, and filling motorcycle cops nice leather boots with snow and hiding them in a freezer didn't go over well. I once was even scolded for tossing a rude citizen a quarter and telling him to buy himself a new personality.

Lt. Ford knew how to deliver a good butt chewing too. He would always say, "Never do that again," and Wes and I never did *that* again. It was always something new that we would come up with that would earn us another good scolding. I caught Wes standing and looking at the reflection of his backside in a storefront window after one of these good 'little talks' by Lt. Ford. I asked Wes what he was looking at and he said, "To see if I still had a butt, it's been chewed on so much lately I'm not sure if it's still there."

Wes Vernon not only was a good prankster, but he was even a better victim for a prank. I'm pretty sure I ruined some of his uniforms by hiding a big block of Limburger cheese in his locker one hot summer. Seemed like the right thing to do at the time.

Wes admired a beautiful woman who worked in a jewelry store located on our beat and we made sure that we stopped at the business on our daily round to catch a glimpse of her beauty. We had to go there anyway, so why not? It was a stormy day and the rain was coming down in buckets. I had secretly applied a good portion of black shoe polish on the inside of Wes's hat that he wasn't aware of. We both wore those famous Cabbie-type hats in those days, the same type the NYPD was known for. By the time we arrived at the jewelry store our hats were soaked by rain. The shoe polish was flowing down nicely over Wes's entire face too. He looked a bit like Alice Cooper, the famous weird rock star of the 70's in the middle of a concert, with all the prince of darkness make-up on his face. Of course, Wes was as charming as always as he said his "How are ya's" to all the staff at the jewelry store. The people were very kind that day and didn't say a word. They stood as if they were frozen in time with wondrous looks of awe on their faces.

I went along with my own gag and pretended that I didn't notice either. Wes actually was able to have a nice conversation with the pretty gal who graciously pretended to flirt back and never let on that anything was amiss. As we left the jewelry store and walked through the streets of downtown, Wes turned many heads and probably frightened a few. After strolling around on our beat for awhile Wes finally saw his reflection in a store window and stopped to see if it was really him he was looking at. He didn't say a word. He just turned and looked at me, as he always did when he knew I had 'punked' him, and simply just stared at me in silence. It was his way of saying, "One day, somehow, someway, I'm going to get even, so you just wait." It was hard for me to take him seriously, especially with black shoe polish dripping off the end of his nose. Life was good.

Sometimes the best thing you can do is make good memories today so that you can have good laughs tomorrow.

Officer Wes Vernon and I liked excitement just as much as the next guy and often assisted medics responding to calls in the downtown area. We were very helpful holding up I.V. bags, clearing crowds and doing what we could.

On Christmas Eve one year we went to assist medics who had responded to a call where an elderly woman was found dead in her downtown apartment. It was determined that it had been a natural death, so we told the medics they could leave and we would wait for the coroner to arrive. The dead woman looked very peaceful on the floor of her living room and I was thinking she must have been a nice lady because most people look terrible when they're dead. Anyway, like most holidays the deputy coroners were busy doing their thing, so we spent a great deal of time waiting for one of them to respond. During our boredom we began looking closely at the many family photos on the walls of the woman's humble apartment. It appeared that the old woman had many people who loved her and many living relatives.

While we were waiting someone knocked on the door. Believing the coroner had arrived, we opened the door to find a small group of high school kids instead. They looked quite festive with their big holiday smiles and their hands full of wrapped presents. One of the kids said that they were here to see Granny Smith to wish her a Merry Christmas. The group had adopted Granny Smith through their school or church group as their favorite grandma. My partner, Wes, had opened the door, so the 'You catch 'em, you clean 'em' rule went into effect. After quite a bit of uncomfortable mutters, Wes finally told the group that Granny Smith was unavailable. "Is she all right? Is everything okay? Why are you here?" came the many questions. Wes continued to fidget, but managed to send them on their way wondering why we were there. I think they had some idea by the look on their faces, but it's a big no-no for cops to disclose a death without the coroner's approval.

It then dawned on me that Wes and I had left our patrol car still sitting in the middle of the street with its overhead emergency lights on. I volunteered to go down and move the car, and on the way down an idea once again popped into my head, maybe not a good idea, but one that would help us, well at least me, to release

73

some of the stress of the situation. After parking the patrol car I went to a small business nearby where I knew the employees from years of working the downtown area. They also knew Officer Wes and knew he was my partner in pranks. I looked up Granny Smith's phone number and had one of the ladies at the business call Granny Smith's apartment and pretend she was a granddaughter. The conversation was captured over a speaker phone and I was amazed how well the participating lady performed the part.

"Is Granny Smith there? Who are you? Why are you at my granny's apartment? Is there something wrong with Granny? (Fake, but convincing sobbing.) Wes bought the cow but held his own. As uncomfortable as he sounded I'm sure he was exhausted after the call, maybe not my best prank.

The last prank I played on Wes cost me a few bucks. I paid for an advertisement in a local newspaper during a summer month when garage sales and estate sales were at their peak. ESTATE SALE, EVERYTHING GOES, ANTIQUE FURNITURE, ANTIQUES, ANTIQUES, ANTIQUES. SUNDAY 7:00 A.M. NO EARLY DEALS (along with Wes's home address).

It was not quite 6:00 a.m. and my son and I were on the way to Wes's house to set up balloons and signs to help folks find the big Estate Sale that Wes didn't know he was having. When we got to the house we discovered that the balloons and signs weren't needed. I had to stop a distance away because of the large crowd that had gathered in the neighborhood around Wes's house. There was a line of people, at least four wide, from his front door that stretched down his walkway to a sidewalk and then down the street a good distance. There were people peering in several windows of his house and pointing at Wes's furniture trying to claim their booty. The people were in an Estate Sale frenzy.

Wes had gotten to bed late the night before, and was probably still in bed sound asleep and surely would be awakened by the noisy horde of people outside. My son and I drove quickly away and never looked back. To this day I still look over my shoulder and wait for his revenge.

Finally, the best pranks were always directed towards the guys who looked so sharp, the motorcycle cops. The motor-cops wear the nice shiny boots that reach up to their knees. They are always sharply dressed, well groomed, and have the expensive sunglasses and cool black leather gloves. Motorcycle cops don't have to respond to the menial calls such as barking dogs, the drunk sleeping in a public restroom, and the likes. While Officer Wes and I did our best to keep the motor-cops humble, it was a resourceful patrol officer we had to take a bow to, his name was Officer Sean Callahan.

Officer Callahan loved to hunt and he was one of those guys that ate what he killed. At the same time, he was an animal lover and a very kind man. One Sunday morning Officer Callahan was out on patrol when he accidentally hit and killed a cat that ran out in front of him. It was a big, fat, orange tabby that looked like Garfield the cartoon character, only real...and real dead. Officer Callahan couldn't find the owner of the cat and didn't want to leave it in the middle of the road so he stuck it on his 'cow catchers' (front bumper push bars on police cars) and drove around with it on the front of his cruiser. I'm sure it must have been quite a sight.

Right, wrong, or indifferent, Officer Callahan brought the poor dead cat to the police department where he proceeded to skin it like a deer. He then stuffed its cheeks with wadded up newspaper and stretched it over a motorcycle cop's helmet that was sitting on top of a locker at the department. It sort of looked like a big Davey Crockett coon-skin cap with its tail hanging down the back, except for the fact that it was just a big orange pussy cat.

The finished product got the nod from Callahan's shift as a pretty clever gag and a resourceful use of a dead cat. Officer Callahan replaced the modified motorcycle cop's helmet to where he got it and went home and probably fell asleep with a smile on his face.

The cat cap never caught on for style and nobody said a word about it to my knowledge. The Statute of Limitations ran out and good ole' Officer Callahan is retired now. If anyone asked me if this really ever happened I'd deny it. So I'll leave it at that.

There is something about a lengthy graveyard shift that sometimes brings out odd behaviors in cops. Many cops don't sleep well during the day, so by the time they get near the end of their busy night shift, they can be a little strange. They see so much craziness and deal with so much bizarre human behavior, I think that they sometimes go to great lengths to mock life itself.

CLOSE SHAVES

CHAPTER THIRTEEN

Seems like every time that I was involved in a shooting, I was the last one to draw my weapon.

On one occasion my partner and I were at a big summer festival keeping our eyes on a large group of opposing gang members, tensions were high and it looked like it could explode into a huge gang fight at any moment. The summer festival was a popular community event that drew thousands of people to the downtown waterfront each summer.

The gang hostilities were growing more intense and Officer Wes Vernon and I could tell that something big and bad was about to happen. We watched about twenty Asian gangsters spread out to position themselves in a wide circle around a very large group of black gangsters and some of the local wanna-be's. There was a mixed crowd with about two hundred innocent teens standing in the middle and hundreds of citizens standing around outside of the circle.

The strategies used by the Asian gangsters were far superior to any others, and I suspect they were expecting to be drawn into the fight. Fortunately they never were, but if they had been, it would have been even uglier.

I could feel the tension rise between the black street gangsters and watched them throw hand signs in the air praising their gang affiliation. At the same time, they displayed hand signs that showed disrespect to their rivals. My partner and I had spread out and were calling for more troops to break up the bomb that was ready to explode. I saw four gangsters about thirty feet in front of me standing side by side looking my way, and then suddenly two others appeared and started shooting in my direction. Two gang bangers from separate gangs standing directly beside me were shot. Amazingly, several other bullets passed by me and through the thick crowd without striking anyone else. One bullet barely missed an infant in a stroller on the other side of the crowd.

The sounds of the gunfire caused instant chaos in the large crowd. I stayed with the gunshot victims while my partner chased the group of gangsters down a nearby road. One of them dropped a .357 magnum revolver as he was running away. My partner, Wes Vernon, was fearless and being a former bull rider, he had plenty of grit. What Wes wasn't aware of, was that while he was chasing the gangsters, he had about a hundred more of them running behind him. Wes was in a foot race with the local gangsters to catch the rival gunmen and he only had about a twenty-foot lead. Anyone watching who didn't know the whole story would have thought Wes was in big trouble and running for his life.

Eventually Wes's competitive spirit won the hunt. He and a large host of officers from every law enforcement agency in the county rounded up the bad boys not too far away. They turned out to be some out-of-town hardcore gangbangers from Chicago. It might have been beneficial to them if they had paid closer attention to where they were when they opened fire. They obviously didn't know the area, because they didn't know the road they were on was a dead end.

For the most part, street gangsters aren't very well prepared and they don't have very good aim. Like the shooting at this festival, the gangsters usually don't hit the target they aim for. Fortunately the victims they shot were other gangsters and not innocent civilians, they just weren't the *right* gangsters.

People would be amazed to know what goes on behind the scenes in any town, big or small. I think knowing is the reason that Wes and I did what we could to make our work life fun during the short moments we weren't chasing calls. As I write this story I am retired from police work and Wes is still hanging in there and chasing bad guys. I see and read about him in newspaper articles occasionally, and it appears that he still has the gift of catching crooks. There is no doubt in my mind that he is still keeping the motor-cops humble with his pranks and maintaining his sanity by seeing the lighter side of life.

THE NAKED GUNMAN

CHAPTER FOURTEEN

Sgt. Schultz had a steady aim. We had been dispatched to a house late one night where a man was causing a neighborhood disturbance. The man was beating on the front door of the house and yelling obscenities. One of those Fred Flintstone gone bad moments, I guess. Like good cops, we always tried to approach silently and 'blacked out' so we would not make ourselves a target.

We parked down the road a short distance and came to a point where we could see the man who was still ranting and raving in front of a single story house on a corner of the street. He was a big guy and looked like a tough biker and sounded drunk and mad. I whispered to Sgt. Schultz that I would sneak up to the side of the house. Sgt. Schultz tiptoed up behind a car that was parked at the curb in front of the house and we watched and waited a short while to see what was happening. A dim porch light was on and we were barely able to see the burly bad boy and hoped that he wouldn't be able to see us.

I was in deep shadows at the corner of the house when the man spotted Sgt. Schultz out of the corner of his eye. The crazed man started yelling drunken threats at Sgt. Schultz, and since all of the bad guy's attention and anger was directed at Sgt. Schultz, I decided to go for a middle linebacker blitz to blindside the big boy and hopefully send him off his feet.

I believe I was in midair when the man suddenly brought up his right hand with the big surprise, a small semi-automatic handgun. At the same time he brought his left hand up to rack a round into the gun's chamber saying, "Take some of this you *&#^#@ cop."

Have you ever seen one of those Warner Bros. cartoons where the coyote stops in midair after the roadrunner pulls a wammy on him? That is exactly what I looked like. I was in the air and only inches away from the man when I heard, Pop, Pop...Pop, Pop.

Two of Sgt. Schultz's rounds pierced through the man's chest and he dropped to the ground like a big sack of potatoes. The other two rounds went into nothing important.

I landed with my feet straddling the man who was now lying flat on his back looking up at me. He was still alive and had an expression on his face like, "Where did you come from?" I was as baffled as the guy was.

The bad guy sounded incensed when he mournfully wailed, "He shot me! He shot me!" He sounded as if his best friend had just betrayed him and couldn't believe anyone would do something so terrible. I was still a bit puzzled myself about my mid-flight delay and could only offer an unsympathetic, "He sure did."

It was then that I noticed that other than a plain white t-shirt, the man wasn't wearing a stitch of clothing. To this day I'll never know how I missed that initial observation.

The sergeant called for medics as soon as the injured man hit the ground. It didn't take long for the shot man to come to the realization that he might die. He let me know this by repeating rapidly, "I'm going to die. I'm going to die. I'm going to die." I answered every one of his statements with a simple, "No you're not. No you're not. No you're not." I wasn't making a statement, actually I was just hoping.

The silly bugger didn't die either. In fact it was only about an hour later he was jumping up and down on his gurney in a hospital trauma room driving the doctor's nuts. I guess some people are too stubborn to die, some are too brave to die, and some are just too plain stupid.

Either way, in spite of all the television and movies that portray cops enjoying shooting people, it's not true. In real life cops really don't like to shoot anyone. To take it a step further, I can even honestly say that every cop I've ever known has a deep fear of having to shoot anyone.

It's very difficult to explain the feeling a cop has, knowing that the last thing in the world they want to do is shoot someone, yet at the same time they have to be willing to shoot someone. Cops, like firefighters and doctors, are wired to save people, not hurt or kill them. Even firefighters and doctors don't understand the psychological stress of it all because they don't have to wear guns to work.

Many cops are killed every year simply due to the fact that down deep inside they don't want to have to draw their gun and use lethal force. There are at least two hesitations that will get a cop killed: 1) Not drawing and shooting their gun when they should because they fear killing another human-being, 2) Liability. Going through a guaranteed hell of public scrutiny, legal repercussions, and even being turned in by his or her own. Cops police their own and are notorious armchair quarterbacks.

Sgt. Schultz and I shared an important moment in his life. Although he kept in total control and followed the department's procedures with textbook precision, I saw fear in his eyes. Not for the close shave of nearly being gunned down by a drunk idiot, but his fear was what an unsympathetic society has in store for cops who shoot good citizens for no reason.

In America, the terrible truth is that violence is alive and well. Cops see it firsthand and with clear eyes. People who criticize and condemn cops for injuring or killing people generally have no idea what truly takes place in our crazy world. It's always been this way.

MY GUN, YOU CAN'T HAVE IT!

CHAPTER FIFTEEN

DONNY RAY was from the south. He was a hefty 6 foot tall guy
with a nasty drug habit and did not like me. When he wasn't
spending time in jail he was spending his time looking over his
shoulder for cops like me who wanted to keep him there. He was
a thief and always in the middle of trouble. I don't think he spent
a day of his adult life without having outstanding felony warrants
for his arrest. Trouble stuck to Donny Ray like lint on a black wool
coat.

One night I was dispatched to a loud noise complaint at an
apartment. There was music blaring from the apartment complex
that was popular for having big nightly problems. I hiked up two
flights of stairs on the outside of the building and followed the
sound of Heavy Metal Rock and Roll that led me to the correct
apartment. I could hear a crowd of people inside trying to talk
over the loud music and I knocked on the door hard enough to get
someone's attention. "COME ON IN," someone finally yelled from
inside. I considered walking in, but I figured with my luck I'd end
up in a big scrap with more goons than I could handle. I knocked
again. The door flew open and standing right in front of me,
bigger than life, was Donny Ray. I knew Donny Ray was wanted
for some recent crimes and Donny Ray knew that I knew.

Before I could say, 'Goodnight Irene,' Donny Ray sprang out and
jumped on top of me. We both went down swinging.

I spent many hours in training academies learning how to fight defensively. I learned every arm-bar, pain compliance point, wrist lock, and handcuff maneuver in the book. But I always tossed the book out when it was time to survive. There are no rules when it comes time for a knock down drag out fight. For veteran cops, there is no such thing as fighting defensively. A person who is stupid enough to fight a cop is usually desperate enough to kill one and there have been plenty of flags lowered at half mast to make that point. Donny Ray and I were in an ugly fight because smart cops don't fight pretty.

"Ty Richie" taught me how to street fight. Ty was only about 5 foot 5 and couldn't have weighed more than 120 pounds. He was one of the original old school street fighters, not a bully but a fighter. For many years I worked downtown on Foot Patrol and enjoyed watching Ty practice fighting the other street thugs. Even though they were only *play* fighting, they were actually drawing blood and their blows were real. Ty could throw a mean high kick and he wore sharp metal rings on almost every finger that caused some very nasty wounds.

One of the things I admired about Ty was that when he was involved in real street fights, (and he was in many), he never fought anyone smaller or younger than himself. And he never fought just one man alone. Ty would always take on two or more at a time and send them away bruised and bloody. He taught me that if you live on the streets then you have to live by the rules of the streets. I worked on the streets so I adopted some of its rules.

The main thing I learned from Ty was that when you are fighting to survive, anything goes.

DONNY RAY and I started on the top floor and the fight was on. He smelled strongly of marijuana and his eyes looked wild and desperate. We were a pretty good match for strength and neither one of us liked each other, so I knew I was in for a rough go. I was learning just how much Donny Ray didn't like me when he began trying to pull my handgun out of my holster and that got my full attention!

Donny raised the bar and I acted accordingly. I didn't feel a bit of pain from any one of the many concrete steps we rolled down. His hand never left my gun and my hand never left his hand that was on my gun the entire way down. With his opposite hand he was punching me and with my opposite hand I was trying to tear the head off his neck by pulling his long hair back between his shoulder blades.

When we finally came to a stop from our amazing trip to ground level, I found myself on the bottom of the pile. Somehow we ended up at the bottom of the stairs in the parking lot between two parked cars. Donny Ray was on top and we were face to face. For one small instant of time we both looked at each other eye to eye and I have no doubt we were thinking the same thing, "Where are we and how'd we end up here?"

My mind apparently cleared quicker than Donny Ray's, and while he was still wondering what the heck happened, I grabbed him by the throat and slammed his head back and forth against the two cars we were pinned between. Bong! Bong! Bong! Bong! went his head and he finally let go of my gun and I was able to squirm out from under him.

When I crawled out from between the cars dragging Donny Ray behind me, I wrestled him into handcuffs and then turned to face a crowd of stoners that had come down from the party. They were either too buzzed to care what was going on or too high to believe what they had just seen. One of them asked me what was going on. I told them they needed to keep the music down as I was stuffing Donny Ray into the back of my patrol car. They said that wasn't a problem and the party was quiet the rest of the night.

BATONS

CHAPTER SIXTEEN

Guns were never a big deal to me and sometimes I thought they even got in the way. Maybe having a gun strapped to my side made me feel brave. On more than one occasion I responded to big calls where I should have carried one, but realized too late that I had left it in the gun locker at the jail after booking someone. I hated doing that.

Officer Jake Evans and I responded to a call where there was some type of disturbance downtown involving a man with a gun. I was on a police bicycle and Jake was on foot.

The guy saw us and started running and Jake took off after him. He was holding a brown paper bag, but there was no way for us to know what was in it. I caught up to Jake who wasn't far behind the man and jumped off my bicycle while it was still moving. At that moment I saw a semi-automatic handgun skidding on top of the sidewalk in front of us and behind the man we were chasing. Jake must have seen it too and yelled, "GUN!!!"

I recognized the gun. It was mine. Somehow it had propelled out of my holster when I jumped off the bike. I scooped it up while still in motion and put it back in my holster. After catching up with Jake, who was still running, I yelled, "That was my gun!" He looked at me with his eyebrows raised for an instant and yelled,

"What??" I shouted back to him, "Never mind," and we kept on running.

The suspect kept a pretty good pace and I don't know about Jake, but I was losing steam.

There is no mention in the S.O.P. manual about using your baton like a boomerang, but that is just what I did. I'd seen this maneuver on some stupid cop television show back in the early 80's and figured it was worth a try. My good ole' straight stick looked pretty cool when I projected it with all my might. It twirled round and round, skipped off the sidewalk, continued twirling round and round, passed by the man, continued going round and round, and struck the side of a nice BMW parked in a nearby parking lot. "KER-PLONK!" was the sound that seemed to echo throughout the downtown business district. I never did try the 'T.J. Hooker' technique of throwing my baton again. I decided to leave the fancy tricks for those Hollywood folks who enjoy shooting people and such.

My night stick was my best friend and I still have it and keep it as a special keepsake. Looking at it brings back lots of memories. It's made of a dark red exotic hard wood called, Cocobolo. Mr. Stick was the name I dubbed my night stick. We had been in many a bar-brawl and several war protests together. If I were given a choice of having a gun or a baton on duty, I would have chosen Mr. Stick. Mr. Stick was introduced to Mr. Bad Guy on quite a few occasions and was very dependable.

One night a local drunk tried to take Mr. Stick away from me. The drunk was sitting next to a busy street on a sidewalk drinking a bottle of wine in open view of the public. He argued with me when I told him he needed to do a better job hiding the booze when he was drinking in public. When he refused to listen, I grabbed the bottle from him and the fight was on. I tried to push him away from me with Mr. Stick, but he grabbed onto the end of it and held on tight. I pulled Mr. Stick toward me and he pulled it back towards him. I pulled Mr. Stick back towards me and he pulled it right back towards him. This went on for what seemed like a very long time as people were driving by on the busy street watching our little tug-o-war. Eventually I pushed the intoxicated man backward to a point where he tripped over a log used as a barrier in a parking lot and I was able to save Mr. Stick. I was too embarrassed to arrest my drunken sparring partner, so we just went our separate ways and called it a night.

In my opinion, days were simpler when cops had only night sticks strapped to their belts, they didn't have to choose what defensive weapon to use. Negotiating in your mind what choice to make can cause delay in decision making when it comes time to use force. That might be good for the bad guy, but it's not so good for the good guy. But, I guess the way the rule makers figure it, cops are expendable, other folks aren't.

Going from a wooden straight stick, to a hard plastic side handle baton (PR-24), to small metal extendable baton that doesn't appear as threatening to the public, batons are quickly becoming an old police novelty. Their brutal appearance does not go well with the look of the modern day civilized police officer. Plus, their reputation as a weapon used in a famous Los Angeles police brutality case 'caught on camera' in the early 1990's didn't help their cause.

But for me the baton was a great tool and useful for police protection, and if necessary, persuasion. To me, not having the baton is like taking the teeth out of a Pit Bull that you bought to protect your family in the bad neighborhood you live in. What use is a dog that only barks and has no bite?

This is the world that we live in. I wouldn't be surprised that in my town the person who started complaining about police carrying batons owned a BMW.

THE TONE

CHAPTER SEVENTEEN

Probably the best tip I ever had came from the first day of training when I was going through the police academy. I was told that I was invincible. If I was stabbed, if someone hit me in the head with an axe, shot me with a .22, .357, .45 or even a shotgun...I would not die. People only die if they think they're going to die. Bullets will not kill you, especially if they are from the gun of some punk criminal who doesn't deserve the air we breathe. The instructor told us, "You can not, will not, and are not going to die." This was set in my little pea brain and I believed it. I convinced myself that police work was all about survival and I wasn't going to ever die on the job. Unfortunately, there must have been a few creeps on the street that had the same training.

Bad guys on television almost always die when they get shot. In the real world that isn't always true. In the many shootings I witnessed or investigated I learned that if the brain is willing and able, life will go on.

An officer friend of mine once emptied an entire clip from his magazine (13 rounds) into a guy that was charging him with a knife. The guy didn't fall until the last bullet sunk point blank into his skull. The man had planned the attack and his own death in a desperate means called, 'Suicide by Cop.' His will was to live just long enough to make sure the cop killed him. The fact that the man survived the first twelve bullets entering his body while he still moved forward was an eye opener for many cops who, like myself, held a false sense of security that our own guns were certain protection for us.

Head shots aren't always fatal either. A personal friend of mine was standing at the back door of a downtown tavern when a random bullet from a drive by shooter a block away hit him in the head. The bullet did a pretty good job of scrambling his brains and to this day he packs around bullet fragments in his head and seems halfway okay. It's always tragic when anyone is shot to death, but it's a bonus to see someone, like my friend, live through a shooting when in reality they should have died.

When a major event such as a shooting occurred in my city the dispatchers would broadcast a specific 'Tone' to all local law enforcement to get our attention. One day I had a newspaper reporter assigned to ride a shift with me when the 'Tone' was dispatched. It was a shooting.

As police officers we had to entertain the public with what is called the 'Civilian Ride Along Program.' Folks who were curious about what cops did (besides eating donuts) were able to ride along in the patrol car and find out for themselves what some of our duties are and how we served the public. I had planned on taking the reporter to every donut dealer in town but instead raced to the scene of a shooting. Donuts would have to wait.

An estranged husband had showed up at the back door of his ex-wife's house and when she opened the door he shot her in the head a couple of times with his revolver. There were children in the house, which made it that much more tragic.

I was the first officer on the scene and as my wide-eyed reporter-ride-along and I approached the front of the house on foot. Another cop, Sgt. McMann, announced on the radio that he had the bad guy running behind a house about a block away. Since there were plenty of other cops arriving on the scene, as well as emergency medical responders, I sprinted (with the reporter chasing behind) to the location where Sgt. McMann had seen the bad guy. Sgt. McMann snagged the shooter in the middle of a neighborhood street and we cuffed and bagged his hands (brown paper evidence bags) to protect forensic evidence.

There is a police procedure that in the event an injured person appears to be dying an officer should remain at all times with the victim in the event that person makes a statement before he or she dies. This is called a 'Dying Declaration.' A Dying Declaration stands as strong evidence in court trials.

The woman was still alive with two bullets in her head, but it didn't look good for her. Since I was first at the scene it was 'You catch 'em, you clean 'em' again and I was ordered to ride with the medics and remain by the woman's side.

The ranking officer who gave the order never said anything about taking the reporter along, so I looked at the medic van and then the reporter and said, "Hop on in, we're going for a ride." He had a pencil and his little notebook pad with him, but I don't think I ever saw him write down one word the entire day. I'm sure he got more than he bargained for.

Once we arrived at the hospital there was already a trauma team masked up and waiting at the ready. We went straight into an emergency room where the reporter and I had to gown up completely. I guess the doctors thought the reporter was a detective since he had a pencil behind his ear and a notepad.

For several hours we sat in that emergency room and watched as the doctors tried to save her life. She survived, but her life would never be the same. I am sure she had plenty to live for back home and it was probably the same reason I convinced myself that I would never let myself die on the job at the hands of another.

What had started out to be a routine day quickly turned into an adrenaline filled morning. One of the best parts of being a cop was that you never knew what the dispatcher would announce next on the radio. A shooting in progress is always the 'Big Kahuna' for adrenaline junkies like me. Bullets flying were the most exciting moments in my career and the 'Tone' became a beautiful sound to my ears.

HUMILIATION

CHAPTER EIGHTEEN

I'd never hurt a fly just for the sake of hurting flies. I've always been a peace maker and I detest any kind of violence. My father taught me to respect women, but the one thing he didn't tell me was if they swing at you, you'd better duck.

And my dad never told me that a thin woman can pack a punch and her skinny knuckles can hurt as much as a big strong man's. The worst beating I ever took was from a tall slender college gal who was mad because I had just arrested her boyfriend. She beat, kicked, gouged, pulled, and tore at me like there was no tomorrow. Her boyfriend, who was in handcuffs, looked on with pity as if he knew personally what I was going through.

We were right in the middle of downtown in front of the tough street thugs and gangsters I'd worked so hard to gain respect from; every street critter was now watching me get my tail kicked by a girl.

I would grab her long slender arms to try to avoid her fingernails and then, "Umph" a knee would come up and, "Ohhh, man." I'd try to protect myself down low and she'd go back upstairs and try to rip out my eyes. She was like Iron Mike Tyson in a dress.

Somehow the crazy woman took possession of my long heavy flashlight and started beating me with it. Crap that hurt. She then tossed my flashlight to the ground and proceeded to pound on me with her fists. I managed to grab both of her wrists to get her under control and she finally stopped fighting, but then complained that I had roughed her up.

There are some things that I will never understand about women. She showed up at her boyfriend's court hearing and told the judge that I was a brute and had no business assaulting her. When I told my side of the story, the judge, a female, seemed more concerned that the woman had thrown my flashlight after she beat me with it. The flashlight was police property and she had no business damaging public property was the verdict. I felt lucky just to get away with my life.

Prior to that humiliating beating I did not have a very good opinion of women who wore the badge. I knew they made great detectives but was worried they couldn't hold their own on the streets. I had no problem working with female police officers after that. The best way to fight fire is with fire and I never wanted to get burnt like that again.

THINGS AREN'T ALWAYS WHAT THEY SEEM

CHAPTER NINETEEN

It was an early weekday morning and traffic was growing as people headed to work. I was on patrol and spotted a small import pick-up truck parked at a popular restaurant that was not open yet. I noticed the windows of the truck were fogged up. I parked behind the truck a short distance away and walked up to the passenger window. There were two people inside the little truck, a male driver with straggling long hair and beard and a woman sitting in the passenger seat. I had obviously not been noticed because as I stood outside the door looking in, I could easily see both of the occupants injecting Black Tar Heroin into their arms.

I could also see a large ball of heroin in some saran wrap on the dashboard by the woman. I continued studying the interior of the cab looking for the possibility of a weapon, when suddenly the woman noticed me. Without hesitation she quickly snatched the ball of Heroin off of the dashboard and tossed it into her mouth. I swung the door of the truck open and pulled the woman out by her upper arm while yelling at her to spit out the dope. She refused and her eyes widened as she tried to swallow the big black tarry ball. Not wanting her to destroy the evidence and at the same time knowing that she could kill herself ingesting such a large amount of heroin, I immediately grabbed her by the throat and tried to keep her from swallowing, all the while I loudly demanded that she spit out the dope.

The woman stubbornly and desperately refused and just stared at me with bulging eyes and black goo coming out of the corners of her mouth as I continued squeezing her throat. It seemed like I held onto that woman's neck for quite a long time standing in the parking lot alongside a very busy street....full of motorists driving by, staring at the wild scene. Since then I've often wondered how many people thought that I was just some lunatic cop out strangling some innocent woman for not using a turn signal or some other minor traffic infraction.

The fact was that the longer I held onto the woman's neck the more I worried about the heroin soaking into her blood system. I called for medics as soon as I could and pried the woman's jaw open, sacrificing one of my fingers to dig out as much of the drug in her mouth as I could. "Don't you dare bite me," I warned her. She could clearly tell that I meant it.

The woman's vital signs started going downhill not long after medics arrived. She was transported to an emergency room at one of the local hospitals where she went unconscious. It didn't look like she was going to make it, but somehow she did pull through. From the way her body looked she may have been better off dying, God only knows.

The public often see cops dealing with situations without knowing the facts, and since they don't have the inside scoop their perception can be skewed.

Working Foot Patrol has many perks and one of them is being able to walk around the waterfront area where the marinas and good restaurants are located. The boardwalk is an excellent location for sightseeing, taking a stroll, sailors, pirates, and boat loving cops.

One summer day when I was on Foot Patrol at the waterfront, I received a tip from a street kid that there was a young teenage girl on a boat in the marina being raped. The girl was a street kid herself and known for being a heavy drinker. I found the boat and the girl but the perpetrators, three adult men, were already gone. Apparently the men took the girl to the boat and filled her with a tremendous amount of hard liquor and then had their way with her. She was out of her mind drunk, literally out of her mind.

The boat was located at the end of a long slip at a marina in front of a popular restaurant. A large crowd of people eating their meals at tables under big sun umbrellas had no idea what had happened on the boat. I called for medics because I suspected the girl had been a victim of a violent crime and because she was in a dangerous state of overdosing on alcohol.

While trying to coax the girl out of the boat she became belligerent and stormed out onto the narrow slip fighting me. The last thing I wanted to do was fall into the cold saltwater wearing twenty-five pounds of police gear. Drowning is not something most cops have to worry about on the job, but in my city there was that potential.

When the girl refused to calm down and tried to run away, I picked her up off of her feet and tried carrying her to land. This was not a maneuver that I had received in training, but there weren't any options. The dangerously intoxicated girl could barely walk, much less run, and I didn't want her to sink like a rock in the cold bay.

As I awkwardly carried the kicking and screaming girl up the slip I took yet another beating from a skinny knuckled girl. She shrieked and yelled for help and went on and on. There is no doubt in my mind that every one of the folks eating at the fancy restaurant thought I was a crazed cave man dragging my date back to a cave or they would see it as another act of police brutality. I'm sure that there were some who lost their appetite worrying what I was up to. At the time, however, I simply wanted to get as far away from the waterfront as I could with as few scratches and bruises as possible.

The medics strapped the young lady into the ambulance and away they went. She was in and out of consciousness all the way to the hospital. I drove a patrol car to the emergency room and watched the doctor's amazing process of treating an alcohol overdose.

Anyone who would go through this process and then ever drink a drop of booze again for the rest of their life could not own a brain. Two large vacuum style hoses were slowly forced down the girl's throat and into her stomach while she was awake. This is not a natural, comfortable experience. One tube carries a thick black chalk liquid into the stomach and the other tube sucks whatever is in the stomach out.

As the tubes were pushed slowly and carefully down the girl's throat her body arched upward. The restraints on her head, wrists, and ankles tightened to the point that she could go no further. Her body writhed and she gagged helplessly. But there could be no mercy. The tubes had to go down to save her life and all that pain was necessary.

My heart lurched out of my chest as I watched tears stream down from the corner of the poor girl's eyes. She was in so much pain, so frightened, so sad, so, so sad.

There was a lesson I learned from the young teenage girl that day. I realized that sometimes my job was going to be a thankless job. I could do what I had to do, but people would always be watching and not always understanding. Good intent is so often misunderstood. People generally believe what they see and what they hear, or at least what they think they see or hear. For the young girl, I can only hope she changed her life. But if not, at least on that particular day, on my watch, she lived. In her drunken state she probably thought I was going to hurt her or arrest her when all I was only trying to do was help her.

Knowing that the public almost always has a poor opinion about police officers makes the job that much more difficult to deal with. It's hard to feel good about what you do knowing that many people only smile and talk to you because they want to be on your good side to avoid a ticket or legal problems. It's sad that the brave efforts and good work by cops are shadowed by a flawed public opinion. It would be wonderful if more people knew what cops had to deal with and why we do what we do. But life isn't always what it seems is it?

GETTING THE BOOT

CHAPTER TWENTY

Everyone loves firefighters, but not all folks like cops. Many of the folks that say they like cops are only pretending because they're guilty of something. Firefighters get all the good press. Cops do millions of good and brave things that nobody ever knows about, but if they slip-up on one occasion it makes the headlines. Kids love firefighters. Old folks adore them. Firefighters work in new buildings with shiny red trucks. They get free pizza to eat while they watch their favorite movies on big flat screen high definition televisions from their comfy firefighter recliners. What makes things worse, is that I never met a firefighter I didn't like. They're great guys and fun to work with. Jerks!

It happened at a busy intersection of two busy streets at a busy time of the day, Calvin, was walking across the busy intersection and was in the busy crosswalk when he was run over by a semi-truck with double trailers loaded with lumber. When the call came, I was only a couple of blocks away on foot and anticipated the worst.

When I arrived there were already several firefighters and medics on the scene. The big semi truck with its double trailers had stopped in the middle of the busy intersection and was blocking traffic with the back trailer positioned over the crosswalk. The victim had been pulled away from the crosswalk with his lower leg missing. Dozens of motorists and a crowd of pedestrians had gathered around the truck and several were gasping in horror at something that I hadn't noticed. It was a portion of the man's lower leg and foot that got ripped off and was stuck between the duel rear tires of the second trailer. I can still remember it clearly today, a red Irish Setter brand work boot, mans size 11.

At about the time I spotted the mangled appendage, I heard what sounded like a New Years Eve celebration in a nearby restaurant. The restaurant was where the emergency responders had dragged the victim. A too happy, considering the tragedy, paramedic came out of the restaurant with his face beaming and walked over to the stuck appendage and with a big "humph" pulled it out. The grinning paramedic then carried the gross thing by the boot back towards the restaurant like a big trophy he'd just won. Citizens watching this stood horror stricken. They gasped, moaned, and some looked as though they were about to faint.

A firefighter joined the paramedic that had the poor guy's leg and boot and they both laughed together on their way back into the restaurant. The dumbstruck citizens watching this were beside themselves.

I walked into the restaurant and found a hoard of emergency responders standing around the victim, who was sitting on a table with a big drunk smile on his face. It was Calvin, a local drunk who had a prosthetic lower leg and foot. The man who had been driving the big semi-truck was there too, and I think he was happier than anyone else.

I could only imagine how upset the growing crowd of citizens was becoming outside seeing their local heroes behaving so hardheartedly. It then dawned on me that firefighters should have to fall under the same unwritten rule as cops, 'You catch 'em, you clean 'em.' So, I did what I thought was best and slipped out of the restaurant and left all the explaining for the guys with the red suspenders.

It's not uncommon to see emergency responders like firefighters and cops standing together at a brutal scene joking around. Rarely do the results of emergency responses have happy endings like this call did. But even so, removing your mind to humor is better than being traumatized for life.

Calvin had a close call on this occasion, but he wasn't so fortunate the next time he tangled with a truck. Calvin was drunk once again and stepped out in front of a delivery truck in an alley and was killed.

THE LONG TRACK

CHAPTER TWENTY-ONE

I've always heard that smart people never volunteer for anything. That might be so, but life sure would be boring if it weren't for stupid people like me. I volunteered several times to help K-9 Officer Jenson train his policed dog Tex. Tex always scared the hell out me. Anyone walking by Officer Jenson's car would jump out of their boots when Tex let them know they were too close. When I trained with Tex I would be his living chew toy. I was supplied with a thick quilt type body suit with a heavy burlap sleeve on one of my arms. Officer Jenson would have me go somewhere and hide and then he would sic Tex on me. How bloody stupid was that? It was a very freaky feeling listening to Tex trying to hunt me down in dark abandoned buildings and even with my big thick burlap arm protectors, I could still feel his sharp teeth clamping down on me as he dragged me from my hiding place.

Officer Jenson's cue to Tex was, "Go find the cockroach, Tex." All the bad guys were cockroaches to Tex. He loved to find the cockroaches and sink his big teeth into them anytime he had the opportunity.

Tex was the most courageous officer on the police force. He could move a crowd of hundreds of protesters back by simply showing his fangs while letting out a deep threatening growl. Tex's bite was bigger than his bark, and his bark was awesome. He was big, he was strong and he was smart too. When he was thirsty he would stand up at the water-fountain in the hallway of the police department, push a button with one of his paws and lap up water. Some would say this wasn't sanitary but nobody in their right mind would ever try to stop him.

A passenger bus was forced to pull over to the side of the freeway near my city one evening because one of the passengers pulled a knife on a female and assaulted her. The bus driver called 911 and I met him at the downtown bus terminal. According to the bus driver the perpetrator got away on foot and was heading downtown.

I received reports of assaults every day, but for some reason there was something in my gut that said this wasn't over. I called the patrol supervisor and told him that my *mojo* was telling me there was a dangerous man on the loose and that he would show up again. The sergeant knew I had a keen sense about things like this, but all we could do for now was to wait.

Within the hour we received a complaint from a business college that was having a night class consisting mostly of women. One of the students looked out of a ground floor window and saw a half-dressed man doing something very disgusting. The rest of the class also witnessed this.

It wasn't but a few minutes later and a few blocks away that women in a beauty parlor looked out the front glass door to see a man doing the same disgusting thing.

The description of the man in these two incidents was the same, and I knew it was the guy from the bus.

Police dogs are not only intelligent, but they put their whole heart into their job. Most good tracking dogs get very excited and run out of gas pretty quickly. Officer Jenson and Tex were already on the scene at the business college and beginning a track. The track led to the beauty parlor that was uphill and several blocks away. By the time Tex and Officer Jenson reached the beauty parlor the pervert had struck again several more blocks to the east. By this time both Officer Jenson and Tex were growing weary. Tex's tongue was practically dragging on the ground, his heart was pounding, and he had lost control of his bowels. A strong track to a police K-9 is intense and stressful for the animal. Like a Greyhound on a racetrack, the dog gives everything it has. Adrenaline will only carry a dog so far and once it hits the wall it is like watching a train wreck in slow motion. Even so, Tex pushed on valiantly.

Officers listening to their patrol car radios began leaving their districts and started heading our way to assist.

It was the next victim that got everyone's attention. The suspect had forced himself through the front door of a house that he chose at random, stabbed an elderly man with a knife, and assaulted the man's wife. He then fled out the couple's back door.

The best way to contain a perimeter when working a K-9 is to have the officers form a circle around the crime scene within eyesight of each other. After a crime is committed, the amount of time gone by must be considered when judging the size of the perimeter. The area of this crime covered a large residential area, and the suspect was moving quickly on foot, so the perimeter was fairly spread out. Fortunately the city had plenty of cops to go around and law enforcement from five jurisdictions were coming to the rescue hoping to have the opportunity to lay hands on the suspect or see Tex do his good work.

I took a position to the east of the perimeter and was standing outside my patrol car with one ear glued to my radio and the other listening for anything out of the ordinary. I must admit, I was praying that the bad guy would come my way. I had my patrol car's overhead emergency lights on, which is what cops do during a K-9 track to make the bad guys hunker down, so the K-9 can catch up to them.

Not long after Officer Jenson had arrived on the scene at the elderly couple's house he announced on the radio: "Be advised units on the perimeter, the K-9 is on a track and running free." It's a very rare and risky matter when a K-9 officer takes the leash off his dog. This occurs when all other options are exhausted. Officer Jenson was in good shape and stood over 6'4" but his dog was much quicker. Officer Jenson figured that if he didn't let Tex run his track and do his instinctive job that someone might be killed by the suspect. With Tex now free of pulling Officer Jenson along behind, there was no chance the cockroach could outrun him.

It was only a minute later when a frightened man just south of my location ran up to me yelling for help. He said there was a man trying to force his way into his house through a back door. I asked him if there was anyone in his house, and he said that his wife and children were still in there.

I had just broadcasted this information to the rest of the troops when I heard Tex's distinctive barking. The barking was followed by a blood curdling scream of a man in pain. "Thank God," I said to myself. I followed the sound of the growling and screaming and saw Tex on top of the bad guy like a hungry lion on top of a gazelle. I could only watch while Tex tore away at the arms of his captured pray. Tex, like all police K-9's, would only take orders from his human partner. Only Officer Jenson could peel Tex away from the cockroach and it didn't take long before he showed up huffing and puffing and saved the bad guy from being devoured. Everyone breathed a big sigh of relief that the sick man's horrible crime spree was over.

The cockroach only received a few minor punctures to his arms. Unfortunately, the creep sliced Tex's throat with his knife. Medics were called to the scene and transported Tex 'Code 3' so that he could get medical assistance. The bad guy was put in the back of an uncomfortable cop car and transported to jail for his bandages. Our concern for Tex over the violent pervert was obvious, Tex was a hero and the bad guy was a zero in our books.

It was many months later when I received a telephone call from the Attorney General's Office and learned the suspect in this case had a violent past with a long history of crimes and that he had escaped from a correctional facility in another part of the state prior to committing the crimes in my city. I gave my testimony at a special hearing and afterwards the suspect was found guilty and given a life sentence.

K-9 Tex, a hero, my friend, and one of the most loyal police officers I have ever worked with died from common health problems that plague his breed. And even though he was a dog, Tex was the kind of police officer that is needed in the violent world we live in today where respect doesn't come easy. I hope there is a doggie heaven with plenty of cockroaches to keep Tex busy. I think he would like that.

MAYBERRY ON METH

CHAPTER TWENTY-TWO

One day I was given knighthood and the charge of protecting a couple of little rural towns. The smaller of the two we'll call Mayberry. 'Sir John of Mayberry' was my official self-made title. After working in a busy city for many years I found myself in an entirely different world. City cops usually look down their noses at county deputies and small town cops. They think that they are not good enough to do real police work. I was guilty of that fable too. It wasn't long before I found out that county deputies and small town cops are actually the real brave souls.

While working in the city's downtown Foot Patrol beat I was involved in a good physical scrap almost every day and at least one knock-down-drag-out-fight a week. The kicker was that my back-up was usually an arm's length away. Cops love a good scrap and would race to a call for the opportunity to go hands-on. It wasn't like that away from the city and all the bright lights. You are on your own in a small town. If you can't talk your way out of getting your butt kicked you'd better know how to survive. Sometimes it took the Calvary fifteen to twenty minutes to get to you, and that is if they even knew you were in trouble. The portable police radios out in the country were like cell phones and dropped calls for help were not uncommon.

And to make it all the more interesting, there were plenty of bad guys. People avoiding police tend to stay away from the city.

Living in the city gets expensive, especially when you're spending all your money on manufacturing meth and buying it. Plus, cooking the crank puts out a nasty odor so it is easier to hide in the country.

Tweekers are like Zombies. Methamphetamine, so the Tweekers tell me, is the devil's drug that steals the soul. You can walk up to almost any heroin addict and ask them if they are hooked on heroin and they often lower their head in shame and remorsefully admit that they are. You can ask a meth addict if they use meth and they would deny it and then try to rip your guts out with their bare hands. Tweekers are violent and unpredictable people.

Small town police departments have a quick turnover rate. Within a short period of time three officers that ranked higher than me quit, leaving me in the position of 'Top Dog.' Being the highest ranking officer in a police department is exactly the last thing in the world I wanted. I am not a diplomatic man and I don't like politics. I was thrown into Town Council meetings and had to deal with small town mayors and mayor wanna-be's and I did a great job ticking every one of them off.

In the history of my county, amazingly only two officers died in the line of duty. Both were in the jurisdiction I worked and Sir John of Mayberry didn't plan on being Cop Kill Number Three.

As Sir John and as the police sergeant I had four full-time officers and about twelve good reserve officers to keep the peace and protect the rights of the good citizens of my two little towns. My rules were simple. Treat good people like good people, treat bad people like bad people, and if you don't know if they are good or bad then treat them like good people until you know otherwise.

Mayberry was like a little island in the middle of nowhere. A forgotten place filled with poverty, bad guys, and of course some very nice people. It was sort of like Shipwreck Cove and the Tweekers had made it their fortress. There is only one small road leading into the town and one small road leading out. The total population stands at about six hundred fifty human beings including a shocking amount of Registered Sex Offenders.

Mayberry, according to my predecessors, had two huge challenges for me, Mean Jean McDuff, and the Tweekers. Mean Jean was famous in her neck of the woods. She worked at a little tavern in Mayberry called, 'Jack's Place'. Her mouth was so foul that it hurt your ears. She didn't like cops and she hated making milkshakes. She really hated making milkshakes, really, really hated making milkshakes.

Jack's Place had a small area for dining and was open to folks under twenty-one. I recall a family of strangers, probably lost travelers, who stopped by Jack's Place to get a bite to eat. They were a nice family, dad, mom, and a couple of kids. The entire restaurant and bar went dead silent when the dad ordered a milkshake. Mean Jean came unglued and let him have it. "I don't

make *$*)#@! milkshakes. Are you *$%# nuts. Get out of my
*&#!@$ bar.

The first time that I heard about Mean Jean I realized I had to
meet the challenge right away and head on. It sounded like a
great adventure. I figured that if I could win Mean Jean's heart
then I might be able to tame Mayberry. It was a busy night at
Jack's Place when I walked in the front door for the very first time,
everyone in the bar froze in their tracks. You could have heard a
mouse passing gas. Mean Jean squinted her eyes and looked
hostile. "Who the #%@* are you?" she demanded with a growling
low serious voice. I could see and hear the sincerity of her anger.
She didn't like cops and she didn't like strangers and she *really*
didn't like cops who were strangers. I stood my ground, smiled
politely, and replied, "I'm John Weber the new guy, I hear you
make a great milkshake." Mean Jean's lower jaw dropped for a
moment and I could see her gears churning. After a long stare-
down I finally won her over. She smiled and offered me a cup of
coffee. It was the beginning of a great friendship and the
beginning of fixing a broken little town.

The world is full of bullies and people who act like bullies. The
true bullies have their own stories. But for Mean Jean McDuff it
was a matter of survival. She was no different than many cops
who act tough simply to stay alive. True bullies don't last long as
cops, but then again, if they show weakness every hungry wolf in
the forest will devour them thinking they are soft.

A ROYAL FLUSH

CHAPTER TWENTY-THREE

Mayberry had a serious drug problem. It was busy as a beehive at night with drug cooking, drug dealing, drug using, and all the behaviors relative to the dark world of Methamphetamine. One day I saw a Tweeker walking through Mayberry who looked like he'd been in a plane wreck. His hand was mangled and wrapped up with bandages. His leg was in a splint and there was a perfect imprint of the butt of an AK47 automatic rifle on his forehead. One of the local drug lords suspected that he murdered another one of the locals (who had been missing for several years) and the drug lord tortured the Tweeker trying to find out where the body had been dumped. In the torture process the Tweek's hand and knee had been crushed. The Tweek didn't want to report it to police, but wanted me to know in the event he turned up missing too.

There was a castle in the fortress of Mayberry that needed to fall. It was a three story house built in the 1800's where large volumes of Methamphetamine were being produced. The king of that castle, Big Jim, had a 45 semi-auto with laser sites and liked to point it at police cars from his upstairs window while we drove by. It was an odd feeling seeing a little red dot on the hood of your patrol car in the middle of the night and we Mayberry cops didn't take it too kindly.

The problem with Big Jim is that he rarely came out of his castle. I'd seen him only a few times outside his house, but he would rush back inside when any cop was near. He had his Zombie girlfriends bring him what he needed from the outside world and didn't have any need to leave the old dilapidated house. But, Sir John had a plan.

It was New Years Eve and every one of my reserve officers came out to play. We borrowed some officers from another little town and met at the Mayberry police station to coordinate a perfect bluff. My plan was to have a monstrous mock police raid on the entire Town of Mayberry. The goal was to get Big Jim out of his house and hopefully catch him moving some of his dope to safety.

It was no secret that everyone and their brother living in Mayberry had a police scanner. We also knew that those with scanners knew that the local police chatted on Channel 3, a limited short-range frequency we used for small talk and not so much for police business.

The plan was this: At 10:45 p.m. sharp we would sneak a fleet of patrol cars into Mayberry from the more hidden and not so popular rear entrance. Those cops would find hiding places in the shadows to watch the most popular dope houses. We would then take our radio traffic to 'Car-to-Car' Channel 3 and make it sound as though we were gearing up for a huge covert drug raid in Mayberry. We would give them the impression we were leaving the front entrance open and hoped it would be the route the spooked dopers would flee to. A small army of cops would be waiting for them as they tried to leave town.

My good friend, Officer Sam Patrick, 'Nine Paul Five' (9P5) and I 'Nine Sam Two' (9S2) started the frenzy:

"9 Paul 5 to 9 Sam 2."

"Go ahead."

"The D.E.A. has arrived, where do you want them to stage?"

"Have them wait at the park on the west side of Mayberry and wait for my cue."

"10-4."

"9 Paul 11 to 5 Sam 2."

"Go ahead."

"The supervisor of the drug unit brought a couple of K-9's, do you want me to go in with them when we boot in the doors?"

"10-4. I have the Warrants with me, I'll meet you on the backside of town at the park, we're using it as a staging area."

"10-4, what time are we executing these Warrants?"

"11:00 p.m. sharp, we're all going in at once from the west entrance to town."

I was hiding in the shadows watching the dope houses down the street when our radio chatter on Channel 3 started up. The bluff worked instantly. Tweekers were running from their houses as if they had caught on fire. They jumped into cars and tried getting the heck out of town as fast as they could. The brave that stayed behind turned off their porch lights and every light in their house.

The king of the castle, Big Jim, jumped into a tow truck that was parked beside his house and he blazed away out the front entrance of town looking as if he'd seen a ghost. He obviously wasn't thinking about the pick-up truck that was dragging behind him without any lights on. And it probably wasn't important to him at the time that his driver's license was suspended as well. These were both excellent reasons for us to make a good legal stop.

Big Jim was found to be holding a huge bag of Methamphetamine and his 45 semi-auto handgun with the laser sites.

The Town of Mayberry didn't have a public sewer system, so some still used cesspools which is similar to having an indoor outhouse. I can only imagine how much dope got flushed down the toilets of Mayberry that night. I'm sure that one day the Department of Ecology will have to condemn the vicinity due to the contaminated ground.

After Big Jim and several others were booked into jail, my cop friends and I invited some of the county deputies to join us in a little midnight parade through Mayberry. With emergency lights flashing, a long line of patrol cars proudly drove slowly through the neighborhoods of Mayberry as every cop laughed their lips off. As we rolled through town and using good ole' Channel 3, I thanked the folks of 'scanner land' for their cooperation and reminded them to D.A.R.E. to stay off drugs and to have a Happy New Year.

Crooks never play fair. Unless the rules told me otherwise, I made up things so that attorneys could test them and politicians could decide if they should make more rules. I certainly wouldn't want to have to supervise someone like me. There are some supervisors who would attest to that. But be that as it may, I retired from police work as a highly decorated officer and kindly referred to as 'Resourceful.'

THE FINAL CURTAIN

CHAPTER TWENTY-FOUR

One of the biggest mysteries about life is life itself and the people in it. Animals are usually predictable, not people. People are amazing. It's astounding how some people who cherish life suddenly and tragically die, and others who take life for granted survive incredible close calls.

Life seems inside out and upside down sometimes. Have you ever noticed that many elderly motorists drive their vehicles as if they have all the time in the world to get some place while young drivers drive as if there is no tomorrow? What is that all about? And when the sun is high in the sky you don't notice it move so much, but when it's going down over the horizon it looks like its sinking fast. Such is life.

A good old and wise friend of mine, Pastor Cecil Thompson, taught me something one day that I will never forget. He had lit seven long candles on a candleabra about an hour earlier and six of them had melted down about one inch. The seventh candle, still barely burning, had melted almost totally down to nothing.

"Do you see how that one candle melted so quickly compared to the others," the pastor pointed out. I remarked, "That's odd, those candles were all the same size when you lit them and they are all from the same box. Why is it that the one candle burned out so fast?" Pastor Cecil's answer was simple, final, and profound. "Because it was meant to." he said with an honest grin. That good man understood death as well as any man could. He had given services at many hundreds of funerals including his own loving daughter's.

Sadly though, some people don't know how to deal with death very well. That's understandable because many of those same people don't deal with life very well either.

Take Charlie for instance. I met Charlie one morning at a bible study. A few of us police officers met on a fairly regular basis at a restaurant in the morning before we went on duty. We would drink coffee, do the traditional doughnut thing, and pray that we would do a good job, stay out of trouble, and make it home at the end of our shift. Charlie came as a guest with one of my cop buddies and I found him to be a very interesting man. He had just been released from spending many years in prison.

Charlie seemed like a very nice man too and was excited about his long awaited freedom. He had the infamous maximum security muscles, was decorated in prison tattoos, had long hair and a thick beard that went down to his tummy. He was hopeful and trying to do the right thing so we all sincerely encouraged him to do well. Our wishes were short lived however, like Charlie's life.

Early the next morning I had just gone on duty and was dispatched to a downtown side street. A woman employee at a business office who had just arrived at work looked out of her window to see a man dragging what appeared to be a dead body down the street. She called 911 and told them what she saw and that he just walked away and left the body in the middle of the street. I figured that it was just a drunk helping another drunk back home. I was wrong.

When I arrived on the scene, sure enough, there was a dead man lying smack-dab in the middle of the street. No one else was around. I had the privilege of attending a special class in the 'School of Hard Knocks' prior to this in the identification of dead bodies. So this time I was able to confirm that the man was really dead. (I believe the name of that class was, You'd Better Be Sure He's Dead 101.)

People don't usually look quite the same when they are dead, but I do recall on one occasion when a dead man was discovered floating in the cold waters of a bay and we had a difficult time trying to find out who he was. It's possible that he had been floating around in the cold salty sound for a couple of weeks. Eventually the Coroner's Office learned his identity. I was blown away when I was told who he was. The dead guy was a local transient that I had dealt with many times. What knocked me off my feet was the guy looked better dead than when he was alive. I didn't even recognize him dead because he looked so good, comparatively anyway. I suppose that the poor waterlogged guy had a lot of practice being dead since he was much like a walking dead man when he was alive. How sad.

It took me a while to recognize that the dead man in the street was Charlie, the man that I had recently had breakfast with. It seemed so unfair. He was like a little canary that had spent most of its life in a tiny little birdcage and then when it was finally set free, a cat sprang on him and ate him.

After the Coroner's Office scooped dead Charlie off the street I started snooping around. In the rear lot of a seedy apartment complex nearby I noticed a familiar car that was out of place. It belonged to a doper who lived on the other side of town. I recognized it from its remarkable dents and rust spots as well as the rear window that was totally broken out. It didn't take long to find the driver of the car. I learned that he was inside one of the apartments, so I went and paid him a visit.

Benny was a heroin addict who spent much of his unproductive life in jail. When he was out of jail he did what dopers usually do for a living and also moonlighted on the side as a snitch. Like most heroin addicts, Benny puked out the truth when I pretended to know what had happened with Charlie. His story didn't surprise me. The old term, "They don't call it dope for nothing," is very true.

Charlie met Benny the night before and talked Benny into taking him to a big city about thirty miles to the north to buy some heroin. Benny had borrowed a friend's car and Charlie had some money. After making the score, Charlie had Benny pull over to the side of the freeway so he could slam the dope into his arm. Charlie needed it now. He had spent many years in prison and the temptation was too great. Only seconds after injecting the sticky black drug into his veins Charlie fell over dead. It was the beginning of a bad night for Benny.

Being the intelligent man he wasn't, Benny did what he thought was best at the time and drove back to his city. The idea of having the dead man sitting beside him in the front passenger seat started getting a bit eerie as the night went on. Benny pulled dead Charlie out from the front seat and propped him up in the back seat instead. There, that seemed normal. Oh, but wait, it even gets better.

It was a nice night and there was a good breeze from the missing back window so Benny and his new dead friend, Charlie, drove back to the big city to the north, then back to his own city, then back to the big city, and then back to his own city again. After driving around for hours, Benny went to the apartment complex and left the cadaver sitting propped up in the back seat of the car in the parking lot. Benny must of had a couple of brain cells left because after a period of time his brain's burned out light bulb eventually ignited and he went back out to the car to get rid of dead Charlie. The owner was on his way to pick up his car and he would certainly discover the surprise in his back seat if it was left there, and chances are the owner of the car would not let Benny borrow it again under those circumstances.

I hope Charlie made it to heaven. Life down here wasn't so good for him. I suspect Benny is probably dead by now. It's hard to say. Either way, I never could muster any hate for anyone who is crippled with addictions. We all have bad habits. Some of us just have habits that are more obvious, that's all. And besides, everybody was somebody's lovable little kid once. To this day when I find myself getting angry at someone, *really* angry, I try to think of what they looked like when they were just a baby being held in their mother's arms. Then I try to picture them as an innocent toddler and then at about a 4 or 5 year old. How can anyone hate a child? And that is all that we really are...just a bunch of big babies trying to survive in this crazy place we call life.

Trying to see bad guys as people who have totally lost their way is one way I coped with dealing with them. No one dreams of becoming a criminal. The world is a tough place to grow up and not everybody is born beautiful with a silver spoon in their mouth. Not everyone has the benefit of being raised in a well balanced home with loving and nurturing parents. It doesn't take much to make one wrong turn and drive down the wrong road and not be strong enough to fight your way back. Why life is good for some and not good for others is a big unknown to me. The mystery of life is life itself. Death has its own mysteries.

A CRUEL REVENGE

CHAPTER TWENTY-FIVE

I didn't want to tell any morbid stories, but this one is so weird that I can't help myself.

It's a story about revenge, desperately cruel revenge. It is a love story, a love story gone wrong. It's a story about a dog. A sad story, but mainly it's a weird story.

In a nice quiet suburban neighborhood lived two women. They had lived together there for many years in a nice clean house. They owned gorgeous furniture and their floor was covered with a beautiful plush white carpet. The women took very good care of their home, especially their nice plush white carpet.

They owned a dog, a big dog. It was an old dog too and very overweight. The big old overweight doggy was like their own child and they loved that dog very much.

One day one of the women did something that deeply hurt the other woman's feelings. The hurt woman became so angry that she decided to take revenge. After writing a cruel letter to her partner, the angry woman went into action. Her devious plan turned out to be a puzzle that took me and the police department's Evidence Technician hours to solve. It wasn't a pleasant puzzle to solve either.

The scene was bizarre. The house smelled of death. There was bright red blood sprayed on almost every wall in the house. Blood had reached nearly to the ceilings in some of the hallways and rooms. The carpet was splattered with blood and a trail of thick red blood could be seen on the carpet throughout the house. Apparently the angry woman decided to kill the poor innocent dog and herself. The dog didn't like this idea. In fact, the dog didn't take kindly to this at all. The trail led from the sofa where the gruesome scene started and ended up back at the sofa where the corpse of an angry woman and her frightened dog were both slumped over soaked in violence and blood under the veil of death.

Apparently after writing a suicide letter, the angry woman carefully spread a bed sheet over the plush white carpet in front of the sofa and then laid another sheet over the sofa. She then sat on the sofa and had the dog come to her. Once the dog was on the bed sheet in front of the sofa she used a large caliber revolver to shoot the dog with the intention of killing it and then herself. The dog had other plans. The first shot didn't kill the dog nor did the second. The dog ran for its life with the angry and now distraught woman chasing after it. The last moments of that dog's life must have been as chaotic as the angry woman's. It was the dog's blood that had covered the walls and the floor. Bloody shoe prints and paw prints told the story. There was no escape for the poor old doggy and the woman finally managed to get it back onto the sheet in front of the sofa. She shot it a third time and then took the next bullet herself. The angry woman probably died much quicker than her four legged pet.

Nothing went right on this day for the angry woman, for her partner, for the poor innocent dog, for friends and family of all involved, for the neighbors, for the police that had to deal with the grizzly scene, and even for the plush white carpet that was ruined.

Suicide, even for revenge, is nobody's friend. It is a road that should never be considered.

They say that a dog is a man's best friend. I don't recall any man ever taking his dog's life in a suicide. Either way I never understood why people have to drag their pets into their own drama. Do you think that dogs enjoy standing in the cold rain while their human masters pan-handle for money? I doubt it, but nearly every one of those sign carrying beggars has their poor dog with them.

Jumpers, shooters, slashers, drowning, asphyxiation, hangings, overdose, I've seen the length people will go to end their life. Every one of these deaths could only be described as truly tragic because most of them could have been avoided. People get desperate at times and forget that the sun is still shining just above the grey skies. Time does heal. Someone really does care. And more importantly, no matter what you have done you can be forgiven.

THE FACE OF DEATH

CHAPTER TWENTY-SIX

Good cops always love to respond to calls such as "Man with a gun" or Robbery in progress" and "40 men involved in a bar fight, *now*." Cops dread calls that involve family members requesting a police check on a relative who has a history of depression or medical problems that hasn't been heard from in several weeks.

Death has a face. I've seen it in every form known to man, it's always unpleasant and always final. As a detective I had to deal with a lot of dead people; children, teens, young adults and old folks. There is nothing like the smell of death. It is distinct and physically sticks to you.

One hot summer when I was a detective, my partner and I responded to a call and went to an apartment complex where a man had been found by his ex-wife hanging by his necktie inside his bedroom closet. He was not in very good shape and even some of the saltiest veteran fire fighters and medics gagged when they entered the complex. I could smell his rotting body from beyond his front door.

My job was to make sure that suicides were not homicides and sometimes I had to actually handle the dead bodies. The air was so thick with death that it was difficult to breath, but I made my feet go one foot in front of the other as if I was treading through a heavy snow storm. As I entered the living room I could see into the bedroom and could see the man hanging in the closet. Several emergency responders were in the house and a couple of them were fairly close to the body.

The man had used the wooden dowel in his closet to hang himself from. Suddenly for no reason the wooden dowel broke and the bloated body fell hard to the floor. Fortunately, I was closest to the front door and had a clear runway to make my escape. While I was quickly running away I looked back to see my partner and the others in the apartment doing their best to hurry out to avoid the stink bomb that was closing in behind them. It looked like a comedy film of a half dozen men trying to get through one narrow doorway at the same time, just like the Keystone Cops.

I will swear under oath that I could actually see a vapor cloud pouring out of that bedroom and then out of the apartment. It took big fans from the fire department to air out the apartment enough to continue our investigation. And it took days for my partner and I to forget that terrible smell so that we could enjoy a meal again.

Within a 24 hour period during my last days as a police officer, I had to respond to a man who fatally shot himself in the chest with a shotgun and another man who literally had blown his brains out with a hunting rifle. I came to the conclusion that I'd had enough looking into the face of death and on that day I distinctly remember telling myself that I'd seen and smelled enough and that it was time for me to go back and join the living after 23 years.

I had watched for many years as the living scurried by me in the streets of my city like ants on a busy anthill. I've watched the seasons come and go like the people I have met. And I've watched the final curtain fall on the lives of many people, even children. I've watched as the last glimmer of light faded from their eyes. This glimmer of light is the life that emergency responders like police, firefighters, paramedics, and emergency hospital staff try to save every day. In order to do so they must find ways to deal with the disappointments. The words 'deal with' are the words that you must understand if you want to understand what cops are made of. They are people, simply people and only people.

Cops are always on duty. And while they are in uniform there is no rest. When they aren't actually busy handling a call they are like minutemen and women ready to spring into action, ready to take a bullet for even the worst creep on the street. It's how they are made. It's why they are appointed. But sometimes, when there is an opportunity to take a deep breath, and if nobody's looking, they do what they can to release some of the tension that is kept secret inside their stomach.

And it is necessary to rid this dangerous tension. Tension is very destructive to our minds and to our bodies no matter how tough you think you are. It is the kind of tension that makes a cop's career and life shorter than most all other careers. It is the kind of tension that wakes us from a deep sleep to a cold wet sweat. It is the kind that keeps our eyes constantly moving from left to right while we are scanning a crowd as we shop at a mall with our family or walk into a movie theater. It causes us to sit with our backs to a safe corner while we eat a bowl of soup at a restaurant with our kids. Cops try to pretend that they are tough but we really aren't. We cry too...when no one's looking.

Most career cops have seen as much violence, human suffering, and death as any soldier on the front lines during wartime. Their good work is often misunderstood and unappreciated and they are aware of this. Yet they must remind themselves daily that what they are doing is right and noble.

This is the 'Cop Story' that people need to know. The other stories can be interesting and even fun, but the fact of the matter is, most people need to know why cops do what they do. The stress of the job is enormous. Cop humor can seem pretty sick and bizarre sometimes, but it's necessary and usually not very harmful to anyone.

If you still aren't buying my message, let me ask you this; "Have *you* ever had to shoot anyone before?"

END

12059545R00079

Made in the USA
Charleston, SC
08 April 2012